Paul Celan

Nelly Sachs

Correspondence

Paul Celan
Nelly Sachs

Correspondence

Introduction by John Felstiner
Translated by Christopher Clark
Edited by Barbara Wiedemann

THE SHEEP MEADOW PRESS
Riverdale-on-Hudson, New York

Published by the Sheep Meadow Press.

All inquiries and permission requests should be addressed to:
The Sheep Meadow Press, Post Office Box 1345,
Riverdale-on-Hudson, New York 10471.

Cover: Rembrandt, "Jacob ringt mit dem Engel." Gemäldegalerie, Berlin.
Etchings by Giséle Celan-Lestrange

Designed and typeset by the Sheep Meadow Press.
Distributed by University Press of New England.

Printed on acid-free paper in the United States. This book meets the guidelines for permanence and durability of the Committee on Production Guidelines for Book Longevity of the Council on Library Resources.

A Cataloging-in-Publication Data record for this book is on file with the Library of Congress. ISBN 1-878818-71-6.

The Sheep Meadow Press gratefully acknowledges grants from the National Endowment for the Arts and the New York State Council on the Arts which assisted in the publication of this book.

Table of Contents

Etching Giséle Celan-Lestrange

Introduction

Gisèle Celan-Lestrange, on 28 November 1984, asked me to accompany her from Paris to the Normandy farmhouse that she and Paul Celan had bought in 1962. There, I'd be able to examine Celan's own library, a huge store of books with jottings and scorings of Europe's most challenging postwar poet. Leaving Paris via the Pont Mirabeau, driving across the bridge, Gisèle took my breath away by saying that it was here her husband had drowned himself in the Seine. In late April 1970, Celan had put an end to a life and work that tested how far an exile's German mother tongue could carry him after the European Jewish catastrophe. On the day Paul Celan was buried, 12 May 1970, his "dear, dear" Nelly Sachs died in Stockholm, having—like him—borne witness to that catastrophe in an exile's unappeasable German lyric voice.

What Celan once said of his mother tongue holds as well for Sachs:

> Reachable, near and not lost, there remained amid the losses this one thing: language. It, the language, remained, not lost, yes in spite of everything. But it had to pass through its own answerlessness, pass through frightful muting, pass through the thousand darknesses of deathbringing speech.

Sachs put it this way: "The frightful experiences that brought me to the edge of death and darkness are my tutors. If I couldn't have written, I wouldn't have survived.... my metaphors are my wounds." And again Celan, calling himself one who "goes with his very being to language, wounded by and seeking reality."

"Sister Nelly" and "Brother Paul," they called each other, during a sixteen-year exchange of letters unlike any other we have—an exchange that bonded them with more-than-familial intensity. Celan's parents had perished at Nazi hands; Sachs's father died in 1930, her mother (to the poet's unnerved grief) in 1950. Each poet was an only child, and though Sachs was a generation older, they found in each other the sibling they'd always craved and an unquestioning need for poetry.

There have been other revealing correspondences between poets in this century—Rainer Maria Rilke and Marina Tsvetaeva, Elizabeth

Bishop and Robert Lowell, yet these letters between Sachs and Celan have a dynamic of their own: a tenderness, a certain desperate fellow-feeling of real survivorhood.

"You know about my things, have them near you," Sachs wrote to Celan in 1957—"thus I have a homeland." That the younger, already recognized poet could cherish her books helped counter her uprooting from her native Germany. Nelly Sachs was born in 1891 in Berlin to cultivated, upper-middle-class parents who felt thoroughly at home in Germany. She grew up in an exclusive quarter and had private schooling. Years later she called her childhood a "hell of loneliness." At seventeen, in love with a non-Jew, she was left by him and suffered severely for two years. An early poem of hers ends: "And life has always tasted like farewell." Her neo-Romantic verse (which she never reprinted) concerned Christmas and Easter, animals and landscape, Mozart, her parents, and she also wrote puppet plays. With the Nazi advent in 1933, Sachs turned toward Biblical themes and Hasidic mysticism, publishing under the newly-founded Jewish Cultural Alliance. After 1938 she was threatened by the Gestapo; the man she still loved, now a resistance fighter, was killed before her eyes. On 16 May 1940 she fled with her mother to Stockholm, aided by the novelist Selma Lagerlöf and the Swedish royal family. She took a one-room apartment with her seventy-year-old mother and soon began translating Swedish poetry into German, meanwhile consecrating her own writing to "the suffering of Israel."

Paul Celan's parents came from Galicia and Bukovina, the "easternmost" reach (he emphasized) of the Austrian empire. His upbringing, though it entailed moderate religious observance and a Bar Mitzvah, would still have left him more-or-less comfortably engaged, like countless other Jews, with western European culture. But Celan underwent a drastic education: Iron Guard anti-Semitism, Soviet occupation, Nazi invasion, ghetto, forced labor, overnight deportation and loss of both parents in Transnistria. Toward the war's end he abandoned Czernowitz (renamed Chernovtsy), spent two years in Bucharest, fled to Vienna, and in 1948 settled in Paris, becoming a translator and above all a poet writing against the grain of a mother tongue the murderers had brutally abused.

The year the war ended, long before they even knew of each other, Nelly Sachs wrote of "Israel's body in smoke through the air," and in

Celan's "Deathfugue" the victims "rise as smoke in the air." The actual moment of recognition occurred in spring 1953, when Celan encountered Sachs's "Chorus of the Orphans" in a French journal, and also "Chorus of the Stones": "We stones...Whoever lifts us / lifts millions of memories." He responded right away with his own harsher lines: "Whichever stone you lift— / you lay bare / those who need the protection of stones." Then for several years the correspondence lapsed.

In 1958, after telling Sachs that her books "stand alongside the truest books in my library," Celan entered a time of trouble from which he would never fully break free. It started with West German papers reporting Nazi criminals in the government, Nazis in South America and Arab countries, and flagrant anti-Semitic slander, vandalism, and violence in the Bundesrepublik. On top of that, Celan at a reading in Bonn found an anti-Semitic caricature placed on his lectern. "All the unanswerable questions in these dark days," he wrote to Sachs in May 1958. Then for seventeen months the only letters are hers. Celan wrote almost no publishable poems, though he was fiercely translating a poet he called "brotherly"—Osip Mandelstam (1891-1938). These translations were also a form of correspondence.

Finally in October 1959, Celan wrote to Sachs—in a broad, hasty hand unlike his usual careful script—about an obtuse and skeptical review of his latest book *Language-Grille.* The same day she got this letter she replied: "Between Paris and Stockholm runs the meridian of pain and of comfort." But a kind of mutual anguish, rooted in loss and loneliness and exacerbated by German neo-Nazism, was beginning to drag down these two survivor-poets. "Oh I know how much I'm burdening you with this," he says, "but I must let you know about it." And she: "I would like to protect you from your own sorrow!"

Poetry, if anything, could lift them. Sachs called Celan's *Language-Grille* "Your 'Book of Radiance,' your 'Zohar'," and he inscribed his Mandelstam collection "To Nelly Sachs the sister," adding in Hebrew—a telling gesture, since he could not at all be sure she knew the language—the exiles' vow from Psalm 137: "If I forget thee, Jerusalem, let my right hand forget its cunning." She answered, "Dear Brother," which must have cheered the man whose poems imagined his lost mother arrested young, like a sister he'd never had. But now three months went by with no letter from him. (In all, there are twice as many letters from Sachs to Celan.) She said she "would like to hear just one word from you."

Because an authentic voice in German was his sole reason for being, Celan's worst wound since the war came in February 1960 when Claire Goll, whose husband he'd befriended and translated in 1949, claimed publicly that he had plagiarized Yvan Goll's poetry. This groundless charge hurt all the more because some German writers took it seriously. These *Menschen,* these "human beings," he wrote to Sachs, "they write *poems!"* It jolted his belief in the moral basis of poetry. With Nelly Sachs herself prey to acute anxieties about anti-Semitism at this time, the two friends were drawn into a vortex. She saw Celan as "the Hölderlin of our time," brilliant and afflicted. Yet that spring of 1960 the prospect of a first meeting lifted their spirits.

The Droste Prize for women poets was to be awarded to Nelly Sachs in Meersburg. But the thought of setting foot again in Germany terrified her. She'd begun suffering from a persecution mania, aggravated by Eichmann's capture, a paranoia of organized terror: "this frightful radio traffic above my house." Resolving to stay in Zurich and cross the Bodensee from Switzerland to Germany only for the ceremony, she asked Celan to join her. "You are coming and then it will be homeland."

"A fairytale here," Sachs wrote to friends from Zurich's Stork Hotel. "At the airport the *Celan* family from Paris, their little son with a giant bunch of roses." Celan had come with his wife Gisèle, a graphic artist, and their son Eric. At this meeting, Nelly Sachs said they might call each other *Du,* the intimate "you." Celan thought (and may have warned Sachs) that the award was a German alibi, was too much philo-Semitism. The next day they spoke "about Jewishness, about your God," Celan later wrote. Sachs said that she was a believer, Celan that he "hoped to be able to blaspheme till the end," and she replied, "We just don't know what counts." That day (it happened to be Ascension Day, in the Christian calendar) she also inscribed a book for him: "It counts Paul it counts / but maybe otherwise than we think." Once back in Paris, Celan dedicated "For Nelly Sachs" the marvelous poem "Zurich, the Stork Hotel." This poem displays their new intimacy and their differing stances within Judaism. Above all it records an epiphany. Looking across the river toward Zurich's great church, together they saw it mirrored in the water that gleamed with gold sunlight. The two poets, knowing the force of light in Jewish mysticism, never forgot this sight.

On her way back to Stockholm, Nelly Sachs visited the Celans in

Paris. He showed her a mix of places: the Latin Quarter, Luxembourg Gardens, Heine's grave, Sainte Chapelle, the Café aux Deux Magots. (As it happens, I was in Paris in summer 1960, and could have passed them in the street. It pains me that I didn't know enough, back then, to be aware of these two.) Again, in Celan's modest apartment, they witnessed a golden radiance of sunlight. But emotions between them fluctuated, the friends reinforcing and then dispelling each other's angst. Later that summer, Sachs underwent a severe crisis amid what she called "Dante-hells" and "Bosch-images." Celan wrote tender, jocular, heartening letters, and sent her a lucky charm, a piece of sycamore bark, adding that her poems would be "even better sycamore bark." When she was hospitalized, he went by train to Stockholm, but was asked to stay at the door of her room. Reports differ on this moment: Did she fail to recognize him? Did she not admit him? To shield herself or him?

Throughout the 1960s these exiles alternately pulled each other up and sank in despair. In May 1961, when Sachs sent her poem "Man is so lonely / searches eastward," Celan responded with a Yiddish expression from his childhood, *zai gezunt,* "Be well!" He would write it out for her "in Yiddish and with Hebrew letters," he said. This pointed memory, and his extra clarity in penning the Yiddish, took care that his once-assimilated coreligionist should absorb the healing words. For Sachs's seventieth birthday on 10 December 1961, Celan sent her an offprint, his "translations from Emily Dickinson, born on 10 December 1830," and he wrote out for her in English Dickinson's quatrain (slightly adjusted):

> who dwelled in Possibility,
> a fairer house than Prose,
> More numerous of windows,
> Superior of doors.

Off and on during the mid-sixties, Celan's depression worsened. He spent months on end in psychiatric clinics, writing brief poems—some lucid, some tortured. For almost two years there's almost no letter from him, so that in 1966 Sachs addressed these lines to

> . . . my Thou
> whom they held prisoner

and whom I was the one chosen to save
and once more in enigmas came to lose
till hard-pressed silence onto silence sunk
and thus a love acquired its coffin then.

"One must not allow oneself / to suffer so," this poem added. But that year the Nobel Prize went to Nelly Sachs and the Israeli novelist S. J. Agnon. Celan decided he couldn't get to Stockholm for the ceremony. A celebration was held at the Goethe Institute in Paris on 10 December 1966. The German scholar Beda Allemann gave a lecture, and Celan, with his carefully prepared copies of Sachs's work, read aloud the laureate's poems. A friend recalls "his trembling voice resonant, somber."

Against her physical and psychic maladies in 1967-68, Nelly Sachs grasped at that apparition of light which she and Celan had witnessed years before in Zurich. "If only the gold would come again through the air out of the mystery." This had been the closest thing to divine presence that the two friends could experience in common. Another shared devotion showed up in April 1968, when Celan sent Sachs a postcard from London (letter #111) of Rembrandt's "Bearded Man in a Cap." They were both attached to this painter who chose to live in Amsterdam's Jewish quarter, used Jewish models, and found his most potent sources in the Hebrew Bible.

Nelly Sachs felt that with Celan she "had a homeland," and both poets dwelt essentially in their mother tongue. "We both live in the invisible homeland," Sachs told Celan in 1969. But later that year he visited Israel for the first time, and sent Sachs a postcard of Jerusalem's Damascus Gate. Celan thrilled to the revived Hebrew language and the free Jewish collectivity, but still felt constrained to return to German-speaking exile in Europe. Maybe post-1967 Israel held more promise than he could meet.

The two poets never saw each other again after those brief encounters in May, June, and September 1960. Sachs had a heart attack, the old terrors of persecution broke out again, and she suffered from intestinal cancer. Celan meanwhile, still gripped by unhealed trauma, was undergoing painful drug and shock therapy. In late April 1970, living alone and out of touch, he drowned himself in the Seine. The news of his absence and death reached Nelly Sachs's bedside. According to the director of Stockholm's Goethe Institute, "she looked at me astonished for a moment and spoke brokenly about his 'going before me'."

The last item of their correspondence, ending a sixteen-year sometimes sacred conversation in letters and poems, has Paul Celan greeting his sister-poet with only this: "All gladness, dear Nelly, all light!"

John Felstiner has published a critical biography of Paul Celan, *Paul Celan: Poet, Survivor, Jew.* Yale University Press, 1995.

Correspondence

1[1]

Stockholm, 5. 10. 1954
Bergsundsstrand 23

Dear Poet Paul Celan, now I have your address from the publisher and can thank you personally for the deep experience that your poems[2] gave me. You have an eye for that spiritual landscape that lies hidden behind everything Here, and power of expression for the quiet unfolding secret. — Now, for my part, I would like to send you my poems *Sternverdunkelung*, unless you know them already. I will ask the Fischer publishing house as soon as I have your answer. A new, as yet unprinted collection of poems is also finished, of which a small selection will soon be appearing in a German literary journal.[3] I, too, must walk this inner path that leads from "Here" towards the untold sufferings of my people, and gropes onwards out of the pain.

All good wishes!
Your Nelly Sachs

2

Paris, on December 13, 1957
78 Rue de Longchamp, 16e

Madam,
I permit myself to come with a request:
You are doubtless acquainted with the journal *Botteghe Oscure*[4] edited in Rome by Princess Caetani. I believe I am right in saying that there is hardly a finer journal of this kind.
Well, the editor has allowed me, together with Miss Ingeborg Bachmann (Munich, Franz-Joseph Straße 9a), to assist her with the selection of the German texts. I thought immediately of your poems, gracious madam. Would it be possible for you to send me some unpublished material* by January 10?
I have acquired your new volume of poems:[5] it stands, with the two others,[6] among the truest books in my library.
Can I hope, now already, to be able to give Princess Caetani some of your poems?

Yours in sincere gratitude and respect

Paul Celan

* *Botteghe Oscure* only prints unpublished contributions; they should remain unpublished until their appearance in B.O.

3

Stockholm, 12. 21. 1957
Bergsundsstrand 23

Dear, esteemed poet Paul Celan,
Your letter was one of the great joys of my life. You know these things of mine, you have them about you: I have a home.
I have therefore thought deeply over your wish that I should send unpublished work; it is such an honor for me.
There are notes and poems from my time of doom lying hidden, just ways of rescuing breath from suffocation. And then came your dear, tender words, and they were a reason to seek things out, write them down and enclose them with this letter.[7]
Do with them as you think best, or keep them for yourself.
May I pass a copy of my new book[8] through you to Princess Caetani and send it to her address?
Your poems live with me. My Swedish poet friend Johannes Edfelt, the best interpreter and translator of German poetry, is writing a series of articles on modern German poetry for Dagens Nyheter, so the Swedish public will soon see your glories unfold as well.

All good wishes and a blessing for your work!

Your Nelly Sachs

4

Paris, January 3, 1958
78 rue de Longchamp

Madam,
Let me thank you from my heart for your poems![9] You do not know how much it means to me to receive poems from you yourself, accompanied by such amiable lines, and to be able to pass these poems on.
I have told Princess Caetani about your book;[10] here is the address:

Palazzo Caetani
Via Botteghe Oscure
Rome

I am sending by the same post the most recent "issue" of *Botteghe Oscure,*[11] as a foretaste of the next (in which your poems will be printed).
Unfortunately I forgot to ask you for a small biographical notice — may I ask you for one now? It need only be a few lines long, mentioning the books you have previously published, including translations.

I wish you all the best, madam!

[12][Shalom Berachah]
Your Paul Celan

5

Stockholm, 1. 9. 1958
Bergsundsstrand 23

Dear poet and dear person Paul Celan,
Once again your letter brought so much joy, but please, call me by my name, it is as if in order to celebrate the miracle of having won someone so far away, one ought to meet without formalities, with the inner essence alone.
Today I received the Autumn 1957 issue of *Botteghe Oscure*. What an achievement, to edit a collection of such spiritual power. How thankful I am that I am permitted to be a part of it. And yet again the best of all is the fact that you are the one who took my things into your care. Until now, in fact, my books have wandered about as orphans. Of course there are a few people to whom I was able to give something through my poems, but otherwise no one wanted to know anything about the things and Fischer had to pulp a part of *Sternverdunkelung*. My new publisher, Ellermann the brave, would not listen to my warnings. For me it is joy enough to have a few friends, but you understand me, dear poet — I still wanted something else. I still have to accustom myself to joy, too, after so much suffering, and when the Swedish poets awarded me their newly endowed poetry prize, I couldn't take anything in and became quite confused, that I, a foreign-language refugee, should be given so much honor.
There is and was in me, and it's there with every breath I draw, the belief in transcendence through suffusion with pain, in the inspiritment of dust, as a vocation to which we are called. I believe in an invisible universe in which we mark out our dark accomplishment. I feel the

energy of the light that makes the stone break into music, and I suffer from the arrow-tip of longing that pierces us to death from the very beginning and pushes us to go searching beyond, where the wash of uncertainty begins. I was helped by the Hasidic mysticism of my own people, which — in this it is close to all mysticism — must ever make its home anew amid birth-pangs, far away from all dogma and institutions.

And now, dear friend, for your enquiries:[13]
born in Berlin '91
Wohnungen des Todes [Dwellings of Death] Aufbau Verl. Berlin 1947
Sternverdunkelung [Eclipse of Stars] S. Fischer Verlag 1949
Eli ein Mysterienspiel [*Eli* a Mystery Play] limited edition Malmö 1950
Und Niemand weiß weiter [And No one Knows the Way Onward] Ellermann München 1957
Translations of modern Swedish Poetry:
Von Welle und Granit [Of Wave and Granite] Aufbau Verlag 1947
Aber auch diese Sonne ist heimatlos [But This Sun Too is Homeless] Büchner Verlag 1957 Düsseldorf

I have some theatrical sketches lying around in manuscript form, and am now working on a further sketch.[14] In "*Abram in the Salt*" I have tried to revive the old devotional theatre [Kulttheater] that incorporated mime and music. *Night Watch* brings the theme executioner and victim into play and in the new one the mythical and the contemporary are brought together. All sketches that may be impossible to perform, but that want to leap out over the edge of poetry. Rudolf Sellner of the Schauspielhaus in Darmstadt[15] encouraged me. I only wanted to tell you this dear friend, just simply so that you know about these things, after all I don't know how long my powers will last.

Live well and the blessing be with you!

Your Nelly Sachs

6 [no date, c. 1. 13. 1958]

Dear Nelly Sachs, admired from the heart!
When your letter came the day before yesterday, I wanted most of all to get into the train and travel to Stockholm to tell you — with what words, with what silence? — that you must not believe words like yours can remain unheard. Much heartspace has been submerged, yes, but as for the legacy of solitude of which you speak: because your words exist, it will be inherited, here and there, as the night is spent. False stars fly over us — certainly; but the grain of dust, suffused with pain by your voice, describes the infinite path.

Your
Paul Celan

7 Stockholm, 1. 29. 1958[16]

Dear Friend Paul Celan,
today [I send] this greeting, which is to tell you that your letter lies among those letters I will never part with for as long as I am alive. They will travel with me on the secret star-ways of my heart.
For a few days a thaw-breeze blew through here. The ice melted. The young poet Hans Magnus Enzensberger came to visit me. He is living in Norway now. And we spoke about you. I am so happy that you and your work are there for the best of the young German generation to look up to in admiration. Alfred Andersch was here two years ago; in those days, too, there were only these voices. That brave man has decided, despite my insistent warnings against provoking the resistance of the listeners, to broadcast my "Eli".[17] I really do fear for him.
Dear poet, dear friend, it is infinitely wonderful to know that you are there!

Your
Nelly Sachs

8 Stockholm, 3. 10. 1958
Bergsundsstrand 23

Dear Friend Paul Celan,
Today a warm greeting from the snow and ice, on the occasion of Hermann Kasack's being here, since your name once again sprang up in such elevated contexts.
I am always happy to know of you and of how your work draws broader and broader circles around it. Below is a minute of dawn for you:

Why this sadness?
This flowing-the-world-to-its-end?
Why in your eyes
the pearling light that dying is made from?

Quietly we slip down this sheer cliff of terror

it gazes at us with star-studded deaths
these dust-stiffened afterbirths
where the song of the birds leaked away
and the lip entombed the wine of speech.

Oh beam that awakened us:
how you took us weary for home
in your darkening arms
then left us alone in the night —

Adieu
Your Nelly Sachs

9 Stockholm, May 27, 1958

Dear friend Paul Celan, a greeting in friendship to you. There are new poems, some forty in number, that sprang up all of a sudden like a gush of blood. Here are some of them.[18]
Would you let me know with just a few words how you are getting on? Whether this letter has reached you? My disquiet is great!

Your Nelly Sachs

Etching Giséle Celan-Lestrange

10[19] Paris, May 30, 1958

Dear, esteemed Nelly Sachs!
I thank you, I thank you from my heart.
All the unanswerable questions in these dark days. This ghostly, mute not-yet, this even more ghostly and mute no-longer and once-again, and in between the unforeseeable, even tomorrow, even today.

Ever
Your Paul Celan

Our three-year-old boy[20] now sprinkles bread crumbs outside for the birds: "Venez moineaux! Venez pigeons!" [Come here sparrows! Come here pigeons!]

11 Stockholm, 9. 11. 1958
but also without a date quite elsewhere

Line like
living hair
drawn
death-night-darkened
from you
to me

Rained in
outside
I bend over
thirsting
to kiss the end of all distances.

The evening throws the springboard
of night over the redness
lengthens your promontory
and I set my foot fearful
on the quivering string
of a death already begun

But such is love!

My beloved friends Giselle[21] and Paul Celan,
yes, it was a joy to hear through Lenke[22] who is so near to my heart, about you, who have so long been profoundly united with me outside all the lands one lives in. She was so filled with joy about this meeting. Ah, you beloved people, those are the invisible rays that sustain us, through all distances — to know of each other. The wonderful print[23] dearest Giselle (is the first name right?) came to me and gives my eyes, in its purity and profound strength of line, an exquisite place of rest. Today I will have a narrow silver-grey frame made for it. I stroke it with my fingers and again and again I want to thank you from my heart.
For a time here we were concerned about a young mutual friend, Peter Hamm. He has had an emotional collapse. I once approached his publisher Herr Neske in Pfullingen. Truly, it is always a blessing in our petrified age to come across a human being who suffers and loves what is his through and through, right to the outermost heartrending point of culmination. Did Brigitta Trotzig — she, too, an enraptured one — ever visit you by any chance?
Countless greetings and wishes from Lenke. She will write soon herself.
How can we possibly answer your love? Again and always again with love!

Your
Nelly S.

12 Stockholm [12. 16. 1958]

You dear friends Paul and Giselle Celan!
Every blessing on you for the Feast of Love and for the New Year. At the beginning of next year our new poems will be appearing with the same publisher.[24] What a happy omen! May all the birds over there bring my greetings to your little boy.[25] Ours are flying about hungry and cold outside my window.

Ever
Your Nelly

13

Stockholm, 6. 12. 1959
Bergsundsstrand 23

Dear Paul Celan, I am writing this in a white summer night — just as unfathomable as the polar darkness in winter — just as prone to awaken all kinds of longing for home. So it is natural that my greetings and heartfelt wishes should go out to you and to Giselle with the wishing-well name, whose aura floats over my bed with the silver-grey stroke of her hand.[26] — Over Easter, thanks to an external provocation,[27] I was racked once again by terrible pain, and it still isn't easy to sit up. But how many deaths must we die before the One comes. Once again, my theatrical experiments are rehearsals for breaking through. Through the mimetic-dramatic play in Ur, the moon-city, "Abram in the Salt" breaks through to the invisible God. In "Night Watch" the victim, having become guilty, breaks out of the refuge in the cow-shed onto the difficult path of penitence. In "Samson Falls through Millennia," the man still suffused with divine creative power breaks into the shallow standardised existence of today and out again into the universe of the soul — and in the short mimetic scenes of "The Magic Dancer," written in recent difficult nights, this breaking out is demonstrated through the body. Far from space-ships and rockets, "It's time to fly with our body alone."[28]
Dear Paul Celan, dear Giselle, I long for a word from you!

Your
Nelly Sachs

"Flucht und Verwandlung" [Flight and Transformation] has reached you, hasn't it?

14

[July 1959][29]

Dear Paul Celan, once again, it is you I have to thank for a rare meeting.[30] We spoke of deep matters in common. You were always present. And Giselle's picture[31] listened in its silver.

Your Nelly S.

15 Stockholm, 7. 29. 1959

Dear Paul Celan,
how nice it was here — you sent a young brother.[32] When will you come?

Your Nelly Sachs

16 Stockholm, September [3] 1959

Dear Paul Celan,
Your "Book of Radiance," your "Zohar"[33] is at my place. I live within it. The crystalline angels of letters[34] — transparent in spirit — still active in the creation — momentarily. I am outside on the threshold, kneeling full of dust and tears — but through the cracks it comes to me, through the gate that leads into the secret in the act of veiling, the first act of creation. In the time when God went into exile (tsimtsum)[35] to create the world out of his inner self. May all your breaths continue to be so blessed that they draw in the moral countenance of the world.

Your
Nelly Sachs

17 Stockholm, 10. 22. 1959

Dear Paul Celan,
Two handwritings are left for me in the world in which the letters glow. If a word comes flying up to me like that, even the worst day is redeemed. One of these handwritings belongs to my friend Gudrun, who saved my mother's[36] life and my own. The other belongs to you. Throughout almost eight years in a Germany bristling with betrayal this one human being was enough to keep the balance. Then you came with the holy word.
The great generosity of the Princess[37] has thrown me into consternation. It is such a very great honor and joy to be allowed to contribute to this wonderful book[38] and now this large unexpected gift.[39] I am going to send my letter of thanks to the rue du cirque (if I read correctly) and then ask permission as well to send in some poems by Rudolf Peyer and Werner Reinert, who asked me if I would.[40]

Please give my greetings to your wife Giselle, from whose hand comes the breath of silver in my room,[41] and greetings to the little boy![42]

Ever your
Nelly Sachs

18 10. 26. 1959

Dear Nelly Sachs,
Thanks, heartfelt thanks for your letter.
Ah, you have no idea of the situation in Germany these days. You see — oh, I know how much I burden you with this, but I have to let you know — of the latest of my experiences. (Perhaps you can show both, the critique[43] and my response, to Erwin Leiser.)

From my heart
Ever
Your Paul Celan

And no one answers these fellows! Even that — answering — is left to the Jew. The others write books and poems "about it"...

19 Stockholm, 10. 28. 1959

Paul Celan, dear Paul Celan,
blessed by Bach and Hölderlin, blessed by the Hasidim. Your letter went straight to my heart. During the last summer, I too had my eyelid raised,[44] I, who am so afraid of lightning-flashes. Your letter — it flashed through me — the name of this critic[45] was brought to me by a young poet[46] who came after a visit by this friend. — At that time a hope in which I had been gathering my innermost strength was dashed to pieces — I fell ill, so badly was I struck. Dear Paul Celan, let us keep reaching across to each other with the truth. Between Paris and Stockholm runs the meridian[47] of pain and comfort.

Ever your
Nelly Sachs

P.S. Erwin Leiser is returning from a journey in the middle of November, I will let him know then.

20 October 31, 1959

Dear, dear Nelly Sachs,
Thanks, heartfelt thanks for your letter!
And now here is the letter that Blöcker addressed to me... (A German writer with whom I am friendly[48] urged him *to do it...*)
You know the "old tune:" of course he has "his Jew,"* of course he rejects my "insinuations" etc... Only one word, such a simple word, eludes him: I am sorry, I can see what I have done...
As if I would feel offended "as a Jewish author"!
Dear, good Nelly Sachs, may I now ask something of you? You wrote in your letter that a young German poet had visited you in Stockholm after visiting Blöcker; could you, please, tell me which German poet it was[49] and what he had to report (perhaps even, as I inferred from your letter, specifically with regard to Blöcker's antisemitism). That Blöcker is lying seems to me evident from the content and tone of his letter; but I would also like to know what you think, dear Nelly Sachs!

Always your Paul Celan

* I know this Werner Kraft, who *lives in Jerusalem*(!).... A sorry figure, not just as a poet...

21 Stockholm, 11. 3. 1959
Bergsundsstrand 23

Dear, wondrously deep, poet Paul Celan,
I inhale your work when I go to rest in the evening. It lies beside me on the table and when the night is too hard to bear, the lamp is lit and I read again.
The connection with Blöcker amounted simply to the fact that Peter Hamm showed me the book "Wirklichkeiten" [Realities][50] which he had received from him with an inscription. But he mentioned to me so many names of poet friends, so that I who know of little when it comes to German literature, paid scant attention, and when your letter came it jolted my memory. How right you are, when you write that

only the words: "I am sorry" elude him — the only thing that should follow when a wound has been inflicted. I am struggling desperately myself against the discouragement that can overcome one after bitter experiences, but you dear friend, with whose work I can compare nothing in purity and depth of vision, I would like to shelter you from your own sorrow!

Always your
Nelly Sachs

22 Stockholm 11. 11. 1959

Dear brother, dear Paul Celan,
You were able to grant me such comfort, such joy — the death-month November is glowing with it! Mandelstamm again[51] — from the family of the deep-eyed. How you raised him out of the night with all the landscape of his language, still moist and dripping from the source. Wonderful event. Transformation — and another new poem is with us. This is the highest art of translation. With my own attempts — in Spring my anthology of Swedish poetry is due to appear in Switzerland[52] — I often fall prey to deep doubts. Will I be able to pass on the polar light locked in its crystal, even after contact with my unquiet blood? An attempt — nothing more.
If only I could give you something of beauty, ah! it would be something supremely beautiful — but, as there is nothing to be found, I enclose only these nocturnal stammerings.[53]

Live well — with a blessing!
Your Nelly Sachs

23 December [19] 1959

Dear brother and friend Paul Celan,
May the New year be blessed for you and yours! With your poems you have given me a homeland that I had thought at first would be seized from me by death. So I hang on here.

Your Nelly Sachs

24 [Stockholm] 1. 12. 1960

Dear, dear Paul Celan,
I send you a greeting, a deep one, over the bridge that connects. You are so deep in my thoughts. The miracle of the Valéry translation,[54] the majesty of your speech. It is there — it will remain!

Your Nelly Sachs

25 [Stockholm] 2. 14. 1960

Dear, dear Paul Celan,
I'm worried to think of you in this time of darkness with your sulphurous epiphanies — immersed in mourning — I would like to hear just one word from you and want you to know how deeply I am bound to you and to your healing speech!

26[55] February 20, 1960

Nelly Sachs, dear Nelly Sachs!
I thank you, I thank you from my heart! Cruelty comes daily into my house, daily, believe me.
What must we Jews yet endure?
And we have a child,[56] Nelly Sachs, a child!
You have no idea how many should be counted among the base, no Nelly Sachs, you have no idea!
For it is not only indolence, it is baseness and cruelty.
Should I name names? You would stiffen with horror. Among them are some that you know, and know well. You don't know how much friendship I have squandered on these human beings (human beings?)!
A few of them even write poems! They write poems,[57] these human beings! What don't they write, those false ones!
Ah, if only I could be near you, speak with you! God protect you!

Always
Your Paul Celan

27 [Stockholm] 2. 27. 1960

Mouth
Suckling at death
and starry rays
with the secrets of blood
leap from the vein
at which World quenched its thirst
and bloomed.

Dying
takes its standpoint of silence
and the unseeing eye
of a wasteland of dust without prospect
crosses the threshold of seeing
while the drama of time
is consecrated
close behind its icy winding sheet.

You are in the world, Paul Celan, the pure man! So the world cannot be entirely dark.

Always
Your
Nelly Sachs

28 [Stockholm] 3. 24. 1960

Paul Celan, dear friend —You have touched the roots of language as Abraham did the roots of faith. The "Parze"[58] is so suffused with your "cargo of light and creation."[59]
I hesitated before enclosing this photo,[60] simple as it is. But it is my room. With the abandoned furniture of earlier refugees, a home-grown rubber tree — and the real treasure in Giselle's silver light.[61] When great weariness besets me I think of Paris and Dresden,[62] both shells for the most beloved of people.

A blessing upon the three of you!
Nelly S.

29 [Stockholm] 4. 30. 1960

Dear Paul Celan,
just a question: on 25 May I am flying with a Swedish friend[63] to Zurich, then on the 29th to Meersburg,[64] then back to Zurich and from June 2 for a week in Tessin,[65] then back to Stockholm. It will be the first journey I have made out of Sweden into a foreign country since the time of my escape. I would never have done it if the doctor hadn't emphatically insisted upon Switzerland. So I shall have the day in Meersburg in between, that leap into uncertainty.
And now I dare to ask: is there perhaps any chance of meeting you in Zurich? Dear Paul Celan, is this possible? Send me word about it. I don't know if one even has the right to ask for such a heartfelt wish!

Your Nelly Sachs

30 May 3, 1960

Our warmest congratulations on the Droste Prize!
Dear, dear Nelly Sachs,
How much I have to thank you for! And now, in a few — easily surmounted — days, I shall have the chance to thank you personally with words that have long been stored up and — may I say it? — in more than one way wrapped in silence and pain.
It goes without saying that I shall come to Zurich, whenever you wish it, please name the day and the hour!
But — don't worry, it is a *happy* "but" — But there is one thing: Frau Waern, who visited us the day before yesterday thinks that, as you are free from your obligations in Sweden, we may ask you: whether you, dear Nelly Sachs, wouldn't also like to come to Paris — to us *and* to Paris?
It's true that we don't live right down in the valley, but rather on the top of five, unfortunately very steep, flights of stairs — may we permit ourselves to invite you to stay with us? But, to be sure, if, as I understand all too well, you would rather avoid this kind of mountaineering, a nice hotel room could easily be found in our immediate vicinity, without a wearisome climb, — I hope you can say yes and come and stay! (Frau Waern also thinks it would be easy to obtain a round ticket

— Zurich to Paris (or Geneva/Lausanne to Paris) would only be a one-hour flight.) — please tell us whether we may expect you! In any case I shall also be coming to Zurich.

From my heart
Your
Paul Celan

31 [Stockholm 5. 6. 1960]

Dear, dear Paul Celan — this joy, this happiness when I found your letter agreeing to come to Zurich. It came just after I had had a series of crushing experiences here[66] — of such a hateful kind that I was very close to a breakdown. Good friends made an effort — but the equilibrium was restored by your letter — as soon as I saw your handwriting. —The date: May 25 depart Stockholm 8.15 arrive Zurich 1.30 I think with Swissair. Eva-Lisa Lennartson, the wonderful reciter of poetry, will be coming too. Ingeborg Bachmann, Dr. Hilty wanted to be there. And you Paul — I can hardly believe it. Not even Germany will be difficult now with the day in Meersburg. From June 2 a week in Tessin[67] and then Paris for a few days? I only hope I shall have the strength for it.

Goodbye blessed poet
Your Nelly Sachs

32 Paris, May 7, 1960

Nelly Sachs! Through this poem I know you. I know you from the Stones' Chorus and from the Chorus of Orphans.
(Both were printed[68] six or seven years ago in the journal "Documents." There I found them. There I found you in them, Nelly Sachs.)

Chorus of Orphans

We orphans
We lament to the world:
They have cut off our branch
And thrown it in the fire —

They have made kindling out of our guardians —
we orphans lie on the fields of solitude.
We orphans
we lament to the world:
In the night our parents play hide-and-seek with us.
From behind the black folds of night
Their faces watch us
Their mouths speak:
We were kindling in a woodcutter's hand —
But our eyes have become angel eyes
And they look at you,
Through the dark folds of night
They gaze —
We orphans
We lament to the world:
Stones have become our playthings,
Stones have faces, the faces of fathers and mothers
They do not wilt like flowers, nor bite like beasts —
And they do not burn like timber when it[69] is thrown in the oven —
We orphans we lament to the world:
World why did you take from us the soft mothers
And the fathers who say: My child you resemble me!
We orphans — there is no one left in the world who resembles us!
Oh world
We accuse you![70]

33 [Stockholm] 5. 9. 1960

Paul Celan, dear, dear Paul Celan, you are coming and then I will be in my homeland, whatever sand we may be standing on. And then, in case I didn't already write it: it is a Swissair plane Nr 251 leaving Stockholm 8.10 arriving Zurich 1.35 in the afternoon on May 25.
Perhaps Gudrun, my life saver, will be allowed to obtain an interzone passport from Dresden, if so she will be in Meersburg on the 29th.[71] Then I would have my two "nearest" by me. I want to do everything possible in order to fly to Paris after the week in Tessin.[72] In the meanwhile we will speak to each other — what a fairy tale! Something

terrible has happened to me here.[73] But I want to forget and try to believe! Now comes the wonderful part.

Always
Your
Nelly Sachs

34 Stockholm, 5. 10. 1960
Bergsundsstrand 23

Paul beloved brother — away now with other forms of address, your letter[74] — is it possible. But I know, I know, a horrific thing happened to me here[75] — of quite a different kind — I became so ill — and none of the friends — except for two, believed! Now I hear from you. Is it possible — human beings — human beings — is it possible! Yes we belong to death in the innermost sense[76] — life has the grace to break us into pieces. It is too late now to go back on the invitation so hesitantly accepted.[77] You know how timid I am, you know, dear Paul, for we know each other well. But I will say the same thing to everyone, I shall fight just as Gudrun once fought for me. I shall do everything, everything for you, you beloved brother!
Andersch[78] was here in Stockholm and invited me to Tessin. But since I will be coming with my Swedish friend,[79] I asked him to reserve two rooms for one week from June 2. In the Hotel Tamaro Ascona. But I shall talk. I shall tell how I received a letter from Claire Goll about a year ago, where she wrote — that she liked my poems and that she had heard that I had been in correspondence with her deceased husband.[80] I had absolutely no clue and wrote in reply: that I was sorry, but I had never known her deceased husband at all and unfortunately had never read anything of his work. But that I would be pleased to learn where his work had appeared, since she had written that she sensed an affinity between us. It was always so cheering, I wrote, to hear of such spiritual relatives. Such was my answer more or less! This is what I am going to tell. I now understand at last why *Aufbau* in New York (Manfred George is my cousin) is so extraordinarily reluctant to send me word about my things. In fact someone once wrote to me that my things always cause a revolution in *Aufbau*. They completely truncated *The Landscape of Screams*[81] — printed it in a completely unrecognisable form. Well, Claire Goll works there as well, of course.[82] So she probably

has something to do with this resistance.
But my dear, my dear — I am so sorely wounded by an experience here — I had thought at last of resting a little in Switzerland, and above all of meeting my life-saver friend,[83] who can so rarely get an interzone passport in East Germany — but what should I say — I believe nonetheless — "everything is for the best." I shall fight for you, much more than I ever could for myself! This business with the Goll letter — is actually the best sign that has been sent to us — to both of us!
I don't know which hotel Ingeborg Bachmann has chosen — and I will not be seeing you directly at the reception — beloved brother — that is bad — for that was a comfort! Giselle — my dear — I shall do whatever I can to come to Paris for a few days!

Your [Eure] Nelly

35 [Stockholm, 5. 11. 1960]

Ah, dear Paul, still reading and reading your letter.[84] Now it is evening. Enquired as to whether the resistance to my things in *Aufbau*[85] perhaps stemmed from the same source, since I too, as I wrote, once received a letter from Frau Goll — there is apparently quite a different reason: *inappropriate* for the readership, say the editors — in spite of my cousin's[86] efforts. Which was sad for me, because I would like to speak to *Jewish* people.
Dear Paul, after these recent experiences I would have liked most of all to close my eyes forever. The solitary man and his sleeping disciples — eternal picture. When we suffer, we cease to belong to anyone but God — that is why our friends abandon us. Be comforted: you hold the balance.

Your Nelly for all time

36 Night of May 12, 1960

Paul, dear you, in the white May night I write this, for I can't sleep when I think of your suffering. Spoke with a reporter[87] who writes articles here in Sweden for several journals, including *Aufbau*. No — there is no literary connection to be found between *Aufbau*[88] and Frau G.[89] She writes fashion features. It is thought that my own things are not suited for a readership that is looking for distraction — they are

too difficult to understand. And also the letter I received regarding an exchange of letters, with the request to gather everything for a publication — was sent to *countless* people. And since I wrote — there must be a mistake, I didn't know I. G.,[90] the matter was closed. This reporter was objective and kind. —
And a *good* thing, too. If I implore my friends and acquaintances to help me in rescuing the Hölderlin of our time from this terrible mayhem — there isn't the slightest degree of self-interest. I shall pray that I receive the strength to wage this struggle for the pure soul!

Your Nelly

37 [Stockholm] 5. 18. 1960

Dear, dear Paul — brother —
of course I will do as you wish[91] and remain silent, but I shall hope in my silence — hope that all is going well. Here in peaceful Sweden I have to endure something awful — nothing to do with literature, no — a shadowy society with a persecutor's methods is up to its tricks.[92]
They booked a room for me in Zurich for the 25th in the Stork Hotel,[93] Weinplatz 2, Zurich.
So we will meet, nonetheless, in hope — in a dark star-time, but still in hope! Rembrandt: "Jacob's Blessing."[94] In the night the blessing blooms upon the wrongly — but for God rightly — blessed man.

Your Nelly

38 Notes by Paul Celan

Joint Stay in Zurich

May 25: Nelly Sachs, Zurich 1, Stork Hotel,
Weinplatz 2
7 o'clock Zurich (the three of us)
9.40 (+ Ingeborg[95] + Hilty)
Nelly Sachs Hotel, Dinner Kronenhalle[96]
(Ingeborg, Nelly, Frau Lennartsson) Max Frisch —
Conversation in front of the hotel
Wednesday: Ingeborg and I are offered the *Du*...
The poem: "You...busy with unlearning the world"[97]

Etching Giséle Celan-Lestrange

May 26: Stork Hotel

4 o'clock Nelly Sachs, alone. "I am a believer, you see." When I then say that I hope to be able to blaspheme until the end: "We just don't know what counts."

May 27: 10 o'clock accompanied Nelly Sachs to the railway station[98]

39

Zurich, the Stork Hotel

For Nelly Sachs

The talk was of too much, of
too little. Of You[99]
and Counter-You, of
how clearness can darken, of
Jewishness, of
your God.

Of
that.
On the day of an ascension, the
minster stood over there, it came
with some gold across the water.

The talk was of your God, I spoke
against him, I
let the heart that I had
hope:
for
his highest, death-rattled, his
quarreling word —

Your eye looked at me, looked away,
your mouth
spoke across to the eye, I listened:
"We
just don't know, you see,
we

just don't know
what
counts..."

Paris, on May 30, 1960

40 [Zurich, 5. 31. 1960[100]]

Paul dear Paul!
My dearest people here together on this sheet of paper, and Giselle and the wide-eyed enchanted child[101] and you were with me all the time and are with me and will be. Right at the beginning[102] your love, Giselle's consecrating kiss — my fear was gone — then Gudrun.

You beloved a blessing — be upon
you — everywhere
Li

From June 2[103]
Hotel Tamaro
Ascona / Tessin

41 Ascona, 6. 1. 1960

You dear ones, dear Paul and Giselle
the fairy-tale continues to come true. We[104] will depart from here on June 13 in the morning from Bellinzona and will be flying out of Zurich at 15.05 and arriving at Paris-Orly airport at *16.15.*
Dear Paul, if you could organize two hotel rooms close to you, it would be marvellous. Then on June 17 I suppose we will fly back to Stockholm. My joy at seeing you again must remain wordless!

Your Nelly

42 on June 8, 1960[105]

Dear, good, happy Nelly,
so we are waiting for your Monday.[106] I hope Paris has everything in store that you expected!
The hotel[107] in which we have reserved two rooms for you is — in the Paris, not the Zurich sense, unfortunately — in our immediate vicinity: five to seven slow walking minutes and some attention paid to the traffic lights when crossing the Avenue Poincaré — Paris will exempt no one from that, not even you... And then of course our five storeys, which...do not lead up into alpine regions. But you are borne up — you will surely be borne up here.
Dear Nelly, in view of possible traffic problems with the present wave of strikes, I will not pick you up at Orly, but at the Aérogare des Invalides in Paris; an airline bus will take you there, and that will be easier for you than a taxi, which can't always be found straight away. I will be standing there and can be recognised by my cheerful impatience.
All my love to you and Eva-Lisa![108]

Your
Paul

43 Notes by Paul Celan

Visit to Paris by Nelly Sachs:
June 13: Nelly Sachs (with Eva Lennartsson)
June 14: Nelly Sachs with Gisèle: Hotel Marthe St Julien,[109] St Séverin, Q. latin, Luxembourg 4 o'clock EN[110]
7 a.m. Luxembourg; Nelly Sachs, Gisèle at home. —
June 15: Nelly Sachs, Eva-Lisa Lennartsson Sainte Chapelle
Montmartre (Pl. du Tertre) Heine's grave
At home. — Fbg. St Honoré, Chinese restaurant
June 16: Marais, Pl. des Vosges, Carnavalet etc.
Deux Magots. (Episode with Max Ernst, who doesn't even offer Nelly a chair)
4 o'clock Enzensberger (also about — infamy[111])
The golden brilliance in the next room
June 17: 2.50 Nelly Sachs departure
Morning Nelly Sachs at our place. The poem "You, busy with

unlearning (?)"[112] among other things [we spoke of] her mother. The mother:[113] for ten whole years every night conversation with the dead, then, in the morning, peace of mind.

44 Stockholm, 6. 18. 1960

You beloved three of mine,
after the departure and then being drawn through the air and then to step out, torn away — but you had hurried before me, the grass on Swedish soil golden-green for one moment, as only in children's dreams. I try to be aware, for I have learnt — picked up one beam shed by your steadfastness[114] — not just to lose myself in pain, in joy, as I — being too hasty — always have. But I still need a little practice, so hard to grasp life outside when one was so at home again after a long time. Friends were waiting and waved and the little flat entered with apprehension was calm and for the moment without evil portents in the air. And I had Gisèle's letter[115] and Paul's picture[116] and my two Bubers.[117] And I put them all among the other beloved things and then I slept and was again with you. And did everything as you wished Paul — I destroyed the letter[118] with eyes closed in the dark radiance of suffering.
And so I hug you and ask blessing for Paul, Gisèle and Eric.

Your Nelly

45[119] Paris, July 1, 1960

Dear Nelly, good Nelly!
I thank you from my heart for your book[120] — for the book and for the words you enhanced it with! Fourteen days have now passed since you have been back up there, up there in your northern home: In the year that is now beginning — because it is indeed beginning *now*, regardless of the calendar year! — is the year of our journey to Sweden: we live for that day.
A book, *Die Judenbuche*, is on its way to you; it was suddenly there a few days ago at the booksellers; I had picked it up while searching for something different — something that, once again as always,

remains the Same[121] — the Flechtheims[122] who had it published are presumably Jews...
It is quiet here. Almost all of those whom your closeness brought closer have stepped back into domains so much their own, so incomprehensible to me, domains where clearness doesn't count as a law. It is one of the most difficult things about our time that so many are falling away from the word — from their own as easily as from the one spoken to them.
It is quiet here. We actually wanted to be in Brittany by now, but Eric has suddenly picked up the measles, and now we are waiting, patiently, until he is fit to travel: ten or twelve days should probably do it.
This morning I received the enclosed letter from Dr. Weber[123] — please give him something: he is making an honest effort.
A greeting from the heart, dear Nelly!

Your Paul

Let us know, please, about your living arrangements.
Please give our regards to Eva-Lisa Lennartsson.

46 [Stockholm, 2. 7. 1960]

Someone stands —
Silence Silence Silence —
nothing more the sun inscribes
and a wreath of sleep grows
about him
who reached up high
higher
until the end.

Sleep grows now in a sandy place
Silence Silence Silence

He oh he
leaves his sand
unwoken
cosmos takes his breath away
his
who let his garland fall

reaped by the sickle of God —
Man-marked
the sand sleeps
a legacy bequeathed by love —

Silence Silence Silence —
when forth the one reaches

the bud sprouts in the salt.

For Paul!
from Nelly

And then:
for my beloved three all blessings for the summer!

Li

47 [Stockholm] 7. 3. 1960

Just now your dear, dear letter, Paul (you must have received mine with its words for you[124] at the same time), I only hope Eric is well again, his eyes always sparkle at me even here right into the midnight sun. Enclosed is the poem for Herr Weber[125] that I sent to him directly but another copy for you. I have nothing here — all manuscripts are packed — since I am probably leaving for the countryside on the 15th. Things are not good here in the house, but the Jewish community has allowed me to make an exchange.[126] But that can't happen until Fall. In reality I am always living with you. Walk through your rooms, rest there when things here are so full of unrest. I dearly hope that you will always stay well for me until we see each other again. Parting is so hard and de-parture a torn-apart word of which one piece was left on the railway station. Gisèle, you dear sister, Paul — Eric — stay well!

Your Nelly

48[127] "Kermovan," Trebabu par le Conquet (Finistère)
— until the end of July —
on July 20, 1960

Dear Nelly! Dear, good Nelly!
we have been in Brittany for eight days under clear skies in a little house on the edge of a huge park grown just wild enough for hares and so also for people. The sea is close by, the people we meet simple and friendly. Each day, as always, our thoughts make their way to you. And you? I am sure you cannot ride a bike as well as Eric — very few people can! — that, I suppose, is why you have to write poems. Which, I feel bound to tell you, is not nearly as hard. Because, as you know, one doesn't ride oneself, because there's always someone to lend a hand, especially when it's uphill riding, and because there aren't only two wheels, but several together, usually five. And does riding in such a fashion also take one to out-lying farm-yards, where one can see piglets who have just come into the world? Sometimes, you say? But surely only under exceptional circumstances, in a leap-year, for example... What? We are in such a year? Well then, let it last for goodness sake, don't just leap into reverse! We do the same, which is to say: we rely on you! We know that we can and may rely on you.
With heather and centaury, with honeysuckle and foxglove and broom-bush (not stinging furze)

Your Paul[128]

49 Stockholm, [7.] 22. [1960] 11 o'clock [telegram][129]

Already feeling much better
Your coming now not absolutely necessary

Nelly

50 [Stockholm, 7. 25. 1960]

Paul my dear,
just a few quick lines
A Nazi spiritualist league[130] is using radio telegraph to hunt me with terrifying sophistication, they know everything, everywhere I set foot.

They tried with nerve gas when I was travelling. Been in my house secretly for years, listening with a microphone through the walls, so I want to give Eric a part of the compensation money, the other part is to go to Gudrun in my testament, that's why I am writing so hastily. I have the proceeds from my parents' property[131] to give away. The testament has to be altered as quickly as possible.[132]

51[133] Paris, on July 28, 1960

My dear, dear Nelly!
You are feeling better — I know.
I know it, because I can feel that the evil that has been haunting you — that haunts me also — , is gone again, has shrunk back into the nothingness where it belongs; because I feel and know that it can never come again, that it has dissolved into a little heap of nothing.
So now you are free, once and for all. And I too — if you will permit me this thought — am free beside you, with you, as we all are.
I am sending you something here that will help against the little doubts that sometimes come to one; it is a piece of sycamore bark. You take it between the thumb and the index finger, hold it very tight and think of something good. But — I can't keep it from you — *poems*, and yours especially, are *even better* pieces of sycamore bark. So please, start writing again. And let us have something for our fingers. You know how much we — and we aren't the only ones — need it.
And if you would like me to come to Stockholm in order to learn a few new Swedish dialects, please do tell me that as well. But: I can imagine that if I came, it wouldn't only be on account of those dialects.

From all my heart
Your Paul

Eric sends you a glass window he painted himself — made of real, genuine glass![134]

52 [Stockholm] 7. 29. 1960

Paul, you loved ones Giselle Eric —
What a joy, your letter, the glass window, the bark, ah, I feel my strength returning. I thought it would never happen. I still shudder from time to time, but Astrid,[135] who has taken me into her care, does everything to help me out of the abyss. Inge Waern was helping me before.[136]
I am so happy that things are going better for you, you loved ones. Gudrun is coming shortly. And in the autumn Paris, my soul![137]

With profound love Your Nelly

53 [Stockholm, 8. 8. 1960]

Paul my dear, how are you and Gisèle and Eric. Please write to me express post, I worry so much. Gudrun is here with me and a dark net has closed around me.

Only please write soon
please, please
Your Nelly

54[138] Paris, on August 9, 1960

Nelly, you dear heart, you are worried, you ask us how we are —
We are well, Nelly, truly well. Let things be as well for you, Nelly, please! There are so many friendly hearts and hands about us. See, please, how close they are, how many they are!
Yes, it is light again — the net, the dark one, has gone away — hasn't it Nelly, you see it now, you see that you are in the open, in the light, with us, among friends?
Yes, you see it, Nelly, as I do, as we do: we can breathe and exist unimpeded, you and we and the many friends all about us.
And I can see the words waiting for you, Nelly, the words that you will inspirit with yourself and the rays of your new clarity — to the joy of us all.

Always your Paul

55 Paris, on August 11, 1960

My dear, my good Nelly!
Frau Wosk rang us the day before yesterday and enquired after our welfare on your behalf — : thank you for your sisterly goodness, thanks from the heart for this being-near and being-with-us of yours! It is quiet here, Nelly, quiet, even when Eric — who is no more capable than his father of writing continuously — comes riding through the rooms on horses and camels — and sometimes, in which case there is bleating instead of neighing, on one of those mountain goats that ate from his hand in the Upper Pinzgau, that is to say in the "land of horses and cows;" he chose for very understandable reasons to make friends with some of them a year ago. I myself am then obliged, whether I wish to or not, to travel on goatback through the landscape, which in view of the furniture, I mean the *mountains*, is no easy task. But I have already learnt a great deal, I am making progress, believe me, Eric will certainly confirm that for you! From time to time we rest, and I am then allowed to return to the Esenin poems whose translation,[139] thanks to Eric's instruction in riding, is also making progress, not at full gallop perhaps, but at quite a respectable speed at least.
And you, Nelly? Now Gudrun is with you, the expected, the helpful one, and you have much to say to each other, with old and new words, under skies that are always clear. I am watching you, I am watching you both, I grateful from my heart that I may.

Always your Paul

56 [Stockholm, 8. 16. 1960]

Paul, Gisèle, Eric, beloved family,
Thanks, my deep thanks for the two post-cards,[140] the comforting angels. I am not in the open yet, Paul, the net of fear and terror that they threw over me hasn't yet been raised. But Gudrun[141] is my comfort here. And you are [as] well. With these two comforting remedies of the only medicine, I hope to overcome all the pain that awaits me or to find quiet release, I long so much for my beloved dead ones. May every one of your days be blessed!

Your Nelly always

57[142] On August 19, 1960

My dear, my good Nelly,
thanks, heartfelt thanks for your letter! You are still in such distress and you find, you dear, you still find words — no, *word-gifts* for us!
Nelly, dear one! I can see that the net is still there, it can't be taken away by the wave of a hand... And yet: it *can* be removed, it *can* and *should* be removed, for the sake of all those to whom you know you are near, for the sake of your nearness, of *your living nearness*! You have your hands, you have the hands of your poems, you have Gudrun's hands — take, please, take ours as well! And take whatever is a hand and wants to be helpful and remain helpful through you, through your being, through your being-there, and being-at-one-with-yourself and being-at-one-with-yourself-in-the-open, take it, please, let it be there, by virtue of this being-able-to-come-to-you-today-and-tomorrow-and-for-a-long-time!
I think of you, Nelly, always, we are always thinking of you and the life you have bestowed! Do you still remember, when we spoke for the second time of God, in our house, the one that is yours, that awaits you, how a golden light shimmered on the wall? Through you, through your nearness, such things become visible, there is need of you, need of you on behalf of those to whom you feel and think you are near, need of your being-here and being-among-people, there is need of you for a long time yet, your gaze is sought after — : send it, this gaze, back into the open, send your true, freedom-bringing words with it, entrust yourself to it, entrust that gaze to us, who also live, who live-with-you, let us who are already free be the freest of all, the ones standing-with-you-in-the-light!
Look, Nelly: the net is being drawn away! Look, Nelly: there is Gudrun's hand, she has helped, she is helping! Look, there are other hands helping! Look, yours is helping too! Look: It is getting light, you are breathing, you are breathing freely. You will not be lost to us, I know it, you will not be lost to us, we know it; with all that is near to you, with all that is near from so far away, you are there and here and at home and with us!

with deepest, heartfelt thanks
your grateful Paul[143]

58 [Stockholm, 8. 19. 1960]

Dear Paul, Gisèle, Eric —
Gudrun is leaving here at the end of August and it would be a heartfelt wish of mine if you could meet her here for at least one or two days. Could you perhaps come on August 27 or 28? Because my friend Frau Wosk will be entrusted with the task of booking a hotel room for you (it is otherwise very difficult to get rooms in Stockholm on account of all the congresses). You will be my guest, with *all* that that implies; I can do that now, it's my greatest joy. If Gisèle and Eric could come as well, I would be one great step closer to the recovery of my health. Please write express! All blessings upon you!

Your Nelly[144]

59 8. 23. 1960

Thanks, Nelly, warmest thanks for your invitation to Stockholm! I hope my telegram[145] reached you — you will know by now that I am only waiting for a signal from you, that we are only waiting for a signal from you.
How are you today, Nelly? Better, aren't you, much better — we very much hope so.
So please let us know — if possible, by telegraph — when we can come.

From my heart
Your Paul

60 Stockholm 8. [29. 1960], 13.33 hrs [telegram]

Doctor wants you to come on about September tenth
Letter follows Nelly

61 [Stockholm, 8. 24. 1960]

Paul, Gisèle, Eric —
I sent a telegram today saying that the doctor can permit your visit on

about September 10. Gudrun will still be here for a few days. It has been a dreadful time; I have Gudrun to thank for the fact that I have regained a spark of my reason.
Dear Paul, Frau Anna Riwkin-Brick the Jewish photographer, has said you can stay with her. Her husband[146] is the editor of the *Jüdische Zeitung*. She sends warm greetings. Gisèle and Eric your two beloved people shouldn't come at the moment in my dark time. They can come when it's light again.

All blessings for you!
Your Nelly[147]

62 Stockholm, [8.] 28. [1960] 11.35 hrs [telegram][148]

Is it possible Paul to come on September 4 or 5
Have to book hotel room
Answer by return telegram

Nelly Sachs Soedersjukhuset[149] Stockholm

63 [Stockholm] Monday August 29, 1960

Dear Paul, have been trying here in the hospital to book hotel rooms for you by telephone — impossible! Please, please go to a *travel bureau* in *Paris* — my attorney[150] was just here and that was his advice. Whichever day you arrive, you are welcome from my heart. We must talk to each other at last so as to restore clarity! Take a taxi from the station directly to the Södersjukhus.[151] Let me have your reply by telegram. Warmest greetings to Gisèle and Eric. Come as quickly as possible!

Your Nelly

64 Stockholm, [8.] 31. [1960] 8.41 hrs [telegram][152]

Have you reserved a room in Stockholm because the Sankt Erik Trade Fair[153] is on and there are no rooms to be had
Please answer by telegram immediately

Nelly

65 Stockholm, [8.] 31. [1960] 14.34 hrs [telegram][154]

Don't come under any circumstances
There are no rooms in Stockholm
I will telegraph as soon as a room becomes available

Nelly Sachs Soedersjukhuset[155] Stockholm

66 Stockholm-Bromma, 10. 12. 1960
Beckomberga Sjukhus[156]
Avd. 29

Paul, Gisèle, Eric —
write to me quickly, I can see "Morning" after the blackness in which we were all ensnared. I have carried you deep, deep in my heart through all these nights. We have all served, always served our time anew. I learnt that here, for I and all those with me underwent a Baal Shem remedial therapy[157] in the serving of time.

I wait with longing for a word from you

always with love
Your Li

67[158] Paris, on October 13, 1960

My dear, my good Nelly!
I thank you from the heart, we thank you from the heart for your letter. We thank you from the heart for this being-carried-in-your-heart!
It is such a extraordinarily liberating, such a joyful feeling to see you overcoming the difficult thing that has tormented you. There is such a thing as healing! How wonderful!

With love, in the name of the New
Your Paul

Eric has — being an exemplary school pupil... — received a ticket for a free trip on a Seine river boat; today there is no school and Gisèle is off accompanying Eric-the-Sailor. They don't know yet that there is a letter from you — how pleased they will be!

68 Bromma/Stockholm, 11. 4. 1960
Beckomberga Sjukhus Avd. 29

You beloved family of mine, Paul, Gisèle, Eric —
not long now and I will be released from the hospital and move into a convalescent home. Perhaps the night is now over and the watchman is starting to blow the reveille. For eight days the doctor[159] has been satisfied with my condition, for I can now eat again and the worst of the pain is gone. So I won't be needing any more electro-shock therapy. But I will have to change my apartment. The scare with the persecutions is too deeply anchored there. Here in Beckomberga[160] — they had been threatening for years to bring me here — they are all, doctor and nurses, so friendly and kind to me that one almost forgets one is in an insane asylum. You dear ones of mine, I am so glad that Paul managed so well at the prize-giving,[161] I had been so anxious.
If only I had all three of you here for once and could make things as pleasant as I possibly can for you. It was so awful this time for my dearest people — for Gudrun too, I weep to think of it. I embrace you with wishes for all blessings always with love

Your Nelly

69 [Lidingö], 11. 24. 1960

If only I had you here!
Paul, Gisèle, Eric,
discharged from the hospital — soon a half-year will have passed in torment. Am now convalescing here in Lidingö not far from Stockholm in the Skågart. Water before my window & rocks & the boats that go to Finland. In summer you must come to Sweden. I will make it possible!
You dear family of mine. My headaches are much better.

Your Li

70 Lidingö 3 near Stockholm, 12. 5. 1960
Högberga Konvaleszenthem Grinstigen

Paul you dear brother and my whole beloved Celan family
I have waited so long for news — but perhaps I hurt you — before in

Etching — Giséle Celan-Lestrange

my despair, in the midst of my journey through Hell. I was so afraid for you that I sent all those telegrams — but now I have been brought out into the brightness. The clarity that I found on this path of purification is such that I had to reach out my hand to all those who were involved in this unhappy story and took away my belief in everything and in myself (I conceded that my tormentors were right and felt myself to be the greatest of sinners). What is the point of all this fighting against races and nations if people don't even know each other as a person. I feel as if I should apologize so much for having let the people nearest to me into my darkness, especially Paul and Gudrun, and having caused them pain. The most terrible thing had happened to me and I can't find the words to say what in truth was behind the thing that brought me within a hair of mental and physical ruin. Yesterday the manager of the house at Bergsundsstrand[162] was here and assured me that all the terror had stopped, he could guarantee it. They have apparently changed everything completely. Yes but fear doesn't leave a person so easily, despite electroshock. My signature is valid again. It has been witnessed by the doctor so I was able at last to make the alteration and supplement [to my will],[163] which they had refused to witness in the Södersjukhus.[164]

But I do ask from my heart for one thing: as soon as you write that you are in difficulties I will send something immediately. I do know what poverty does, my mother[165] and I always had to take in work, and now the compensation has come[166] and I can help my friends. That is my only true remaining joy.

Enclosed is the new cycle, poems[167] written in November in the Beckomberga Hospital.[168]

Always your Nelly

71 [12. 14. 1960]

In the frozen age of the Andes
the princess in her coffin of ice
embraced in cosmic love
clear as resurrection
with the destiny of the dead
already inscribed
on the root-sinking bent-over gaze —
seeing at night —

untroubled by the elements' longing for dissolution
as far as the father's dark power —

there —   here —
she stands —
distance captured in flesh
signalling shallows
mutely glowing
blind breathing sea-growth —

In the midst of the smoking ark
of the dreams of fear
of all who flee dragging their pasts behind them
she stands —
anointed now
in the midst of the quarrelsome languages
newly raised Babylonian towers
and pyramids dislocated with longing
measured for dying in houses
while time's end always flowing in the ear
brings what remains of the banished

Another one for Paul
from Li

Death still celebrates
the life in you
fool in the coil of haste
each step further removed from the childish clocks

and closer and closer drawn by the wind
the robber of longing
chairs and beds rise in awe
for the unrest has become sea-like

and doors —
the key placed on guard
turns on itself with entrance outwards —

The white sisters bathed in stars
by the touch of the signs from afar
by the one who feeds the veins here
from his subterranean source of thirst
where the visions must drink their fill —

and another one for Paul!

72

Until Dec. 30: Chalet 'Les Fougères, *Montana* (Valais)
on December 23,1960

My dear Nelly,
our warmest thanks to you, our warmest greetings to you — from the mountains.
We are well, Nelly, don't be worried. We really do have everything that we need. The fact that we have everything, that we can offer Eric everything he needs and wishes for is one of the thoughts that help us to cope with the unlovely things that sometimes come from outside. So also is the thought that you now at last have everything to protect you against outward things. Please claim it all for yourself, really spoil yourself — we will be so happy if you do.
Warm thanks for your poems.[169] You are, notwithstanding all your terrible shocks, still yourself, untouched in your innermost essence; you are and will remain the one who in making a gift of herself is bestowed with gifts. It will always be so.
I haven't done very much work; one volume of Esenin is complete, it is due to appear in February.[170]
Perhaps I can send you my Darmstadt speech in January; it is being printed at the moment.[171]
I have a bad conscience with regard to three of your friends, Inge Waern, Eva-Lisa Lennartsson and Frau Wosk: I failed to answer several of their letters. Please tell them how much I regret that. These last months and weeks hardly yielded a word.
All the best for the New Year! Our warmest greetings!

Your Paul

73 1. 6. 1961

And the blind bodies
of the outcasts
are taken in hand by the night
step by step
night that oversprings its own darkness
and led like brothers and sisters
in growing danger
they fall into the catacombs of Ur
groping the buried treasures
that in the candelabras black fire glow
or now with white soothsaying light
or with red now, the Amen of colours —

But the healing happens
on a new path
for way in and way out
can never be the same
when farewell and reunion
are parted
by the incurable wound of life
and the aura of early morning
is the answer and gift of another night —

Paul and Gisèle with as much light
as I can send!
Nelly

74 [Stockholm] 2. 10. 1961

She dances —
but with a heavy weight —
Why does she dance with a heavy weight?
She wishes to be inconsolable —

Groaning she draws her beloved
by the curls of the world's ocean from the deep

Breath of disquiet blows
on the rescuing joist-work of her arms
a suffering fish flounders speechless
in her love —

But suddenly
sleep bends her over
at the neck

Those who are set free
are life —
are death —

The crooked line of suffering
retracing the God-kindled geometry
of the universe
always on the light-trail to you
and darkened again in the epilepsy
of this impatience to reach the end —

And here in four walls nothing
but the painting hand of time
embryo of eternity
with the ancient light on its brow
and the heart the manacled fugitive
leaps for its calling: to be a wound —

Paul and Gisèle and Eric — will you come here this summer? I hardly dare to ask — I long for it so. At the beginning of June I may go to Högberga in the rocky islets of Stockholm to be at Lidingö,[172] and I could rent accommodation in a boarding-house[173] nearby. But we would have to make up our minds quickly because everything will soon be booked out. I have been back in the apartment for two weeks now — have to put everything in order. Wasn't easy — the fear is still inside me. But it is peaceful now nothing is left of the evil — if only it could stay like that — how grateful I would be. You dear ones — my loves I embrace you.

Your Nelly

75

Paris, on February 14, 1961

My dear Nelly,
our warmest thanks for your dear letter and — for your poems.[174]
We would like to have accepted your invitation to spend the Summer in Sweden and with you — we have often thought about it. But unfortunately it won't be possible this year: not only a sister of my father[175] who lives in England, but also Gisèle's mother[176] (she has lived in Brittany for years) are laying claim to their rights — their great-aunt's and grandmother's rights in particular: by which they are referring — understandably — to Eric. So we will have to go somewhere where Britain and Brittany are not too far off.
Take care of yourself, dear Nelly! We all send you our warmest greetings.

Your Paul

Greetings to Inge, Eva-Lisa[177] and Frau Wosk.

76

[Stockholm, 3. 21. 1961]

My beloved family — Paul Gisèle Eric, I send you warm greetings and hope that you are well. I am never quite at rest on that point — but I hope so with all my heart! Magnus Enzensberger is here and is such a comfort for me this week, for next week I will have to return to Beckomberga for an indefinite period.[178] But you don't need to worry — I feel very *well*. Bengt Holmqvist who is one of the finest judges of literature here and loves your poems, Paul, will be coming to Paris in April. Please welcome him when he telephones!

With love
Your Li[179]

77

So lonely is man
searches eastwards
where melancholy appears in the face of the dusk

red is the east from the cocks' crowing

Oh hear me —

To dissolve
in the longing for lions
and the whiplash lightning of the Equator

Oh hear me —

To wither with the childlike faces of the cherubim

at evening

Oh hear me —

In the blue north of the wind-rose
keeping watch at night
already a bud of death on the eyelid

onwards thus to the source —

Paul/Gisèle/
Li
Beckomberga
5. 1. 1961

78

Paris, on May 4, 1961
78, rue de Longchamp. XVIe

I thank you — we thank you, my dear Nelly, for your poem.
In the loneliest hour: I thank you.
I hear you.
In Czernowitz where we lived, the Jews always offered a wish when they said goodbye to each other: Be healthy! [Sei gesund!] That is not a German expression, but a Yiddish one, and so now I permit myself to say once more, in Yiddish and with Hebrew letters:

[Yiddish: Zai gezunt][180]
Your Paul

79 [Stockholm] 7. 16. 1961

Paul and Gisèle my beloved friends —
I am sure you are at the seaside or in the mountains, and here we have been talking about you again and always again my brother and sister. Because Gudrun has come and although I am still in the hospital, she comes to me each day and we go for walks. How good it is to have this soul with me. I hope that we too shall see each other again; that's a heartfelt wish!

Yours ever
Nelly[181]

80 [Stockholm-]Bromma 9. 3. 1961
Beckomberga Sjukhus

Who calls?
My own voice!
Who answers?
Death!
Does friendship perish
in the encampment of sleep?
Yes!
Why does no cock crow?
It waits for the kiss of rosemary
to touch the water!

What is that?

The moment of loveliness
that time fell away from
slain by eternity —

What is that?

Sleep and dying are featureless

Paul, before I return to the apartment in two days — to test — whether I may be allowed to live in freedom again — I send you this new greeting from the hospital — and my wish for blessing upon the three of you — my beloved family!

Nelly

81[182] 9. 13. 1961

My dear Nelly,
It is Jewish New Year — accept our warmest wishes for all the best in this new year. May it bring you everything you long for, peace and health and poems!
It has become very lonely around us, Nelly, we are not having an easy time. But I hope that for us, too, things this year will be different from the last.

With love
Paul

82 Paris, on October 6, 1961
78, rue de Longchamp

My dear Nelly,
thank you for your letters and poems![183] And please don't be angry that I haven't written for so long!
So how are you? We think of you often — we think of you every day.
I am sending under the same cover a little volume of Esenin translations[184] — I hope it doesn't disappoint you. Many years ago, first as a pupil at the Gymnasium, later as a student in Czernowitz, I was much preoccupied with these verses,[185] here, in the West, they came to me again, eastern, with the flavour of home.
I often wish we could speak at length about writing poems, — of that and of so many other things.

Gisèle and Eric send warmest greetings
The warmest from me as well!

Your Paul

83 [Stockholm] 10. 15. 1961

My dear Paul, such joy and happiness your handwriting brought me — much longed-for, very profoundly received. I have been here in the flat for over a month. The benign powers are helping me to try to stand firm. It is hard, but I can once again go out alone and even in the nights it has become better. I am making a great effort to accept with infinite gratitude the freedom that I can have. If the three of you could come sometime — I don't dare to express what that would mean to me! I could rent lodgings for you in a boarding-house[186] — but I dare say nothing more. Esenin is lovely and he shines out of your translation.[187] And my journey into dustlessness, in which all my poetry is gathered will soon be coming to you, as soon as it has appeared.[188] An embrace from my heart.

Your Nelly

84 [Stockholm, 12. 22. 1961]

The mountain climbs into my window
love is inhuman
moves my heart into the brilliance of your dust
my blood turns to granite of melancholy

love is inhuman

Night and death build their land
inwards and outwards
not for the sun
star is an evening-word closed with a seal
torn apart
by the inhuman ascent
of love —

Paul Gisèle Eric
with love and gratitude
Nelly
In December 1961

85 [1962][189]

White in the Hospital Park

I

In the snow
the woman walks
holds on her back
clenched in her misplaced grip
under covers
broken-off branches with buds
still hidden by night

But she quite still in her madness
in the snow
looking about her and wide open
the eyes where
from all sides nothingness enters —
But close under covers the distance
has started to stir
in her hand —

II

The quiet
drenched from so many wounds
religion of the faithful already departed
lives off martyrdom still
always new like Spring —

Paul and Gisèle
always deep in my thoughts!
In refuge again with my gentle protectors![190]

Your Nelly

Eric how are you? Every blessing on you!

86[191] Paris on March 6, 1962

Warm thanks for the poem,[192] dear Nelly! We think of you often, we think of you every day. And wish you, from our hearts, all, all the best!

Your Paul[193]

87 [Stockholm 5. 31. 1962]

Paul — Gisèle — on the day of an Ascension[194] — I am so fond of you — I think of the three of you when things start getting too difficult. I sit in my little room and look out into the hospital park where the birches are at last turning a fine shade of green — I long for you all endlessly — two years ago it was Eric's dark stars that I saw for the first time in Zurich. I long for you so — whatever becomes of me — the love and kindness in the hospital makes the dreadfulness possible to bear. A blessing on the three of you.

Always
Your Nelly

88 [Stockholm-]Bromma 4, 9. 5. 1962

We are weaving a wreath here
some have thunder-bolts of violets
I have only a blade of grass
full of the mute language
that makes the air here tremble

Paul — Gisèle — Eric
You beloved of mine — I've been back here for 8 months.[195] I had to be protected. It was awful. How are you? I have you deep in my heart — always!

Behind the door
you pull at the cord of longing
until tears come
in this well you are mirrored —

Your Li[196]

89 Paris, on September 7, 1962
78, rue de Longchamp

My dear Nelly,
You letter of the 5th arrived this morning and your two poems — warmest thanks!
We too think about you a great deal, again and again. Everything is unforgotten: the letters and poems, the conversations and words that have been exchanged over the years — in Zurich,[197] in Paris,[198] in Stockholm.[199]
Now I want to read all your poems again, read them out to Gisèle, think of what we have shared, of everything.
Perhaps I may add here that a great deal has changed for us — presumably because we are still the same.
We wish you all the best, Nelly, we wish it from our hearts.

Paul[200]

Greetings to Gudrun

90 [Stockholm] 3. 1. 1963

Dear Paul — dear Gisèle — I think of you and of Eric so often and so deeply. How are you. You are always so close to me but the space between is so wide, though it be planted with love. After the year in hospital I have returned to the old apartment. It wasn't possible to get a new apartment. They are doing what they can in the way of rescue, but it is hard, even to be able to exist again. Did you receive the "Zeichen im Sand" [Signs in the Sand]? I have also finished my translations of the 2 great poets Ekelöf and Lindegren.[201] I embrace you with love

Your Nelly

Gisèle your picture[202] hangs on the wall

91 Paris, on 3. 5. 1963
78, rue de Longchamp

Dear Nelly,
we are happy to hear from you yourself that things are better again, that you were able to return to your apartment, that you are working.
You are often present in our conversations.
I received the Signs in the Sand and read it most attentively, as I do everything that comes from your pen. — I thank you.
Allow us all to wish you good things and true!

Warmly
Paul

92 [1963]

And I see your eyes
wide open
entrance to the night
where for the last time
your time
a hanged one
filled your starry pupil —

no one shut
this portal of the soul
Open, it burst into flames
in the blaze of the executioner's pyre

For Paul the brother
On the Day of Souls

93 Stockholm, in November 1963 [11. 4. 1963]

When the great terror came
I fell silent —
fish with the dead side

turned upwards
air bubbles paid for the struggling breath

All words fugitives
to their immortal hiding places
where the conceiving power must spell out
its star-births
and time mislays its knowledge
in the riddle of light —

Paul — Gisèle — Eric
I am homesick for you!

Nelly

Back in the apartment again after years of hospital.

94 Stockholm, 3. 18. 1964

Straight into the utmost
don't play at hiding from pain
I can only look for myself
if I take the sand into my mouth
to taste the resurrection
for you have abandoned my grief
you have departed from my love
you my beloved —

Paul — Gisèle I long to hear from you. Every blessing upon you, for Eric too —

Always with love

Your Nelly

95 [Stockholm] 8. 10. 1964

My dear Paul
what a joy for me your word — your translation.[203] What a gift to the German language. And to me to hear from you!

I have now been at home in my apartment for 1 year and what a blessing: they are letting me live again — sleep — work. 4 years of hospital-night — police protection — self-sacrificing kindness of the doctor,[204] freedom at last.
I have always carried you in my heart — you beloved brother and sister and my heart was beside itself with longing.

Every blessing!
Your Nelly

96[205] Paris, on December 24, 1964

My thanks, dear Nelly, for your glowing riddles.[206] We spend much time in their company, as we do with all your poems, and hope to be allowed to enjoy their company for a long time to come.
Soon it will be eleven years that we have known each other,[207] and a great deal has happened in these years, much of which you foresaw.
In a few days a new year will begin — may it bring you joy, happiness and all fulfillment. Warmest greetings, from Gisèle and Eric too.

Paul

97

Despair
your letters like matches
spitting fire
No one gets to the end
but through the antlers of your words —

Place comfortless
site of sheer madness
before it grows dark
life's stragglers
and first-born of death
without haven

ravenous fever
brushing the secret
of the invisible Messiah
with wild longing for home —

We plunged
into the dungeon of parting
backwards
already black as shadows
poured out
into the void

For Paul, Gisèle, Eric
my beloved family
a blessed year 1966

98 Paris, [10.] 20. [1966] 5.15 p.m. [telegram]

Our warmest congratulations[208]

Gisèle and Paul Celan

99 [Stockholm] 11. 11. 1966

Paul and Gisèle would you come to Stockholm[209] for December 10? I need hardly say that it would be the greatest birthday joy. But if so let me know by telegram, so that we can get tickets from the Nobel Foundation and reserve rooms

Your Nelly

100 Paris, on November 16, 1966

My dear Nelly,
We were touched by your invitation to come to Stockholm for your birthday and for the Nobel prize-giving. But sadly it can't be done because I, having unfortunately taken rather extended holidays last year, am unable to obtain permission for leave from the École Normale, especially so soon after the beginning of semester and so shortly before Christmas.

But in a small way we will be present on December 10, because: on the evening of December 10, in your honor, Beda Allemann will speak about your poetry for 25 minutes in the Goethe-Institute here, and then for some 30 minutes I will read from the books of your poetry.[210]

Gisèle and Eric greet you as warmly as I do

Your Paul

101 12. 8. 1966

My dear Nelly,
please take the enclosed folio[211] as a little sign of our warm greetings and wishes for you.

Paul[212]

102 Stockhom, 12. 30. 1966

Paul, Gisèle, Eric, my dear ones, I wish you a happy New Year. We listened to the tape.[213] At the house of my friends Bengt and Margaretha Holmqvist. It was a most profound experience for us. Bengt Holmqvist and his wife helped me to survive in the terrible years. He is one of the leading literary scholars of the younger generation and he loves your work. He will be coming to London and Paris and will ring you, he'd like to meet you personally. His history of modern literature until the Second World War[214] is also being translated into German.

With love
Your Nelly

103 Paris, January 13, 1967

Over a "Stamperl:"[215]
My dear Nelly, these lines, which, as Bengt Holmqvist was kind enough to recommend, are to be written with a view — among other things! — to his — now comes a word in which *one* of our many landscapes, namely the "post-kakanian,"[216] lights up — , to his (here's the word:)

"Vidimus"[217] — in any case these lines, rambling far and wide and thereby — how else? — striving back towards you, to you and your poems, these lines — what are they doing? They are greeting you, many times over and — what could be simpler? — from the heart.

Your Paul[218]

104 Stockholm, 10. 30. 1967

Paul, dear Paul, your poems[219] breathe with me day and night, and so they share my life. This is the first time since a heart attack at the beginning of the year and long weeks in the hospital that I am able to write to those who are nearest to me, and since the Searcher[220] there has been silence.

Again it is the Holmqvists who have been the rescuers over this whole period. Gudrun was also here with me for a month with an East German permit. How often I have been with you in spirit, and then the gold over the water and in your room![221] Gisèle, you too are with me in the big book[222] with your hand, but how clearly you also stand before me in the sight of my eyes. These days with you all were the last moment of brightness afterwards 3 years of night.

With love from my heart, also for Eric

Your Nelly

105[223] 12. 8. 1967

My dear Nelly,

it was so good to hold your letter in my hands and to be reminded by you yourself of that light that shone over the water in Zurich and then in Paris. Once, in a poem, a name for it even came to me through Hebrew.[224]

And with that my warmest congratulations upon your birthday!

Your Paul

Please note the address on the envelope[225]

106 [Stockholm] 12. 13. 1967

Paul, my deepest thanks for your commemoration. If only the gold would again come through the air out of the mystery. It has been black for us both for so long, I felt for you through countries. Marc[226] is also one of our number. Transparent!

Your Nelly

107 [Stockholm, 3. 20. 1968]

Paul, dear Paul, did a little gold come to you from nowhere, upon my heart I would like to send it to you. —

Nelly

108[227] Paris, on March 22, 1968

My dear Nelly,
thank you for your lines, for the reminder of that light.
Yes, that light. You will find it named in my next book of poetry, which is to appear in autumn — called by a Hebrew name.[228]

Warmest!
Paul

109 Paris, on April 1, 1968

My dear Nelly,
I come with a big request:
You know several of Gisèle's etchings, once you delighted us with a photo[229] in whose background one of these etchings could be seen. Gisèle has done a lot of work in recent years, there is much new work that is beautiful and — permit me to say it — unique in its way, Gisèle has exhibited at various places with success, occasionally even with great success.[230]
Now she is to exhibit in Sweden, very soon, in fact. First she will be participating in three group exhibitions to each of which she is contributing between ten and twenty folios, the first of them will be

opened on *April* 6th in *Skara* and will then go to *Hudiksvale*; a further group exhibition will take place, also in April, at the municipal museum of *Kristianstad*.[231]
From *May* 3 to *May* 25, Gisèle has a *solo exhibition* (some sixty etchings) in the *Galerie Ariane* in *Göteborg*.
My dear Nelly, I am sure there are artists and critics among your friends whose attention you could draw to these exhibitions. Do it, please!
It would be best of all, of course, if you could see to it that a Stockholm gallery brought the Göteborg exhibition to Stockholm — believe me, Gisèle's works deserve it. And there would be the added joy of your seeing them as well.
Please accept my warmest thanks, my warmest wishes, my warmest greetings

Your Paul

On the day after tomorrow I leave for three weeks in England; my address there: Paul Celan, c/o Miss Berta Antschel 41 Tarranbrae, Willesden Lane, London NW6

110 [Stockholm] 4. 4. 1968

Dear Paul, first of all thanks for the joy of seeing your dear handwriting and now for Gisèle as requested the addresses of some of the best international galleries

Galerie Bleu Sturegatan 28 Stockh. Ö
Galerie Burén Sturegatan 24 Stockh. Ö
Galerie Blanche Mynttorget 4 Stockh. C
Galerie Pierre Nybrogatan 1 Stockh. Ö

First these four, which are all particularly interested in France. Though of course they are quite international anyway. Gisèle would do well to send some photos beforehand and to mention the exhibition in Göteborg. I have been so unwell that I can now only bear to be with my small circle.
My dear Paul, you in any case are among those who always dwell in my thoughts as the young brother. Not a word has been forgotten!

Your Nelly

111 London, on 4. 14. 1968

My dear Nelly,
thank you for your letter and the addresses of the galleries — I have passed them straight on to Gisèle. I hope there turns out to be an exhibition in your vicinity. —
Take care of yourself, dear Nelly, and accept my warmest wishes!

Your Paul

I will be back in Paris from April 16

112 Stockholm K[4. 27. 1968]
c/o Rålambshov Sjukhus[232]
Gjörvellsgatan 16

Dear Paul, dear brother,
I have been back in the hospital for some days. Terrible things again all the gold has vanished. Can't write much. But if Gisèle writes to me from Göteborg[233] and lets me know the name and address of the gallery in Stockholm I will write to them and do as much as I can for her.

Always with love
Your Nelly

You know that I am for peace and that revenge of any kind is alien to me!

113 [Paris] on April 29, 1968
45, rue d'Ulm

My dear, good Nelly,
heartfelt thanks for your letter. May your powers return to you swiftly, may your stay in the hospital be as short as possible, may you be at home with yourself and your works and among your friends very, very soon!
Please let me know as often as you can about your state of health!
Gisèle tells me that she has already sent you the invitation — sadly the

Etching Giséle Celan-Lestrange

invitation card was a total technical failure, the design by Gisèle[234] that is reproduced on it has in reality a much, much stronger and more absolute presence — , in any case Gisèle tells me that she has already sent you one of these invitations for the Göteborg exhibition,[235] and one each for Eva-Lisa[236] and Lenke.[237] She is going to send you further invitations under separate cover and is very grateful that you are going to put in a word for her with the Stockholm galleries.
I am sending under the same cover a small Supervielle translation,[238] that I hope you will like.
Get well again soon, dear Nelly!

Yours from the heart
Paul

114 [Stockholm] 5. 2. 1968[239]

Dear, dear Paul, I have asked Eva-Lisa Lennartsson to look after Gisèle and sent her Stockholm address to Gisèle in Göteborg.[240] And I have also written to my cousin Emmy Brandt, who because of her husband[241] has been living for a few years in Göteborg Baldersgatan 10, that she should look after Gisèle. I have also asked Eva-Lisa to get her friend the famous art critic[242] involved.
The doctor[243] is wonderful.

All, all my love
Your Nelly

115 [Stockholm] 5. 18. 1968[244]

Paul, dear Paul, have heard nothing from Gisèle, am quite concerned. Is there to be no exhibition in Stockholm?[245] I've written to so many friends and am back sitting with my gentle friend the doctor[246] and have to be "protected" again. You can presumably imagine how this is connected with certain things in our time. And I who am for peace have to stand up for everything. If I didn't know that you and the friends live here with me on earth, I would have gone under long ago. Dear Paul, to set my mind at rest: Are they leaving you in peace? I hope so, I hope so. A blessing be with you.

Your Nelly

116 [Stockholm, 7. 10. 1968]

My dear Paul, I am writing to let you know that I am back in my apartment after 3 months of hospital, after going through dreadful things. I am always thinking of you for fear lest you not be spared. Am physically so weak with so little blood that I am longing for the end. A greeting and a blessing from my heart

Your Nelly

117 Paris, on July 1968

My dear Nelly,
thank you for your letter.
I am glad that you are home again, I wish you health and poems that are written as they must be.

Warmly
Your Paul

118 Paris, on 2. 5. 1969

My dear Nelly,
my thoughts often make their way to you, joined by the hope that you are well. Today there is the additional question as to whether you could send me a few new poems for the journal "L'Éphémère," of which I have recently become one of the editors.[247] I know one of your French translators, Bernard Lortholary,[248] personally; I would pass the poems to him and then we would look through the translations together.
Or would you like to publish something else, writings, for example? The journal would of course publish the original texts as well, with the greatest care in an appropriate format.
Will you write to me soon, dear Nelly?
I hope so.

Warmly
Your Paul[249]

119 [Stockholm] 2. 10. 1969

You dear Paul
what a joy to hear from you. It is going to be hard to fulfill your wish, but I want to so much since it is for you. Apart from this I haven't written anything since the Searcher.[250] There was that dreadful time in between where they had to protect me. I wrote a few things in order not to go under, but incomprehensible for anyone else because they are haunted by the telegraphic persecution.[251] So I came home and wrote what I am enclosing for you.[252] Know of nothing else. But you understand, we both live in the invisible home country.
Your poems are always by me.
I read them before sleeping in the evening, this is how we pray.

Your Nelly

120 on June 2, 1969

My dear Nelly,
here, at last, is the issue of L'Éphémère with your lovely poem,[253] together with what I believe, and others have told me, is a successful translation by Bernard Lortholary.*
Accept my thanks, also for your patience with me, who am so slow to write letters.
With warmest thoughts

Paul

*Address: 45 rue d'Ulm, Paris 5e, perhaps you could write him a few lines; he would be very pleased.

121 Stockholm, 6. 5. 1969

You dear Paul,
I have come back from the hospital where I underwent a serious operation, thought so much of you, then had the joy of getting your letter and the lovely translation.[254] All the very best

Your Nelly

122 [Jerusalem] 10. 8. 1969

A warm greeting from Jerusalem[255]
All, all the best!

Paul

123 [Paris] 11. 7. 1969

My dear Nelly,
in Tel-Aviv, at a meeting with Israeli writers,[256] I heard from one of them that you have left hospital and are back home. — Take care of yourself, dear Nelly, be healthy.
Have you written anything new? And may I see it?
I would like to receive a few lines from you. I have moved, please note my new address:

6 Avenue Zola, Paris 15^e^
(Telephone 828-92-78)

I have finished another book of poems, it is due to appear next year in June,[257] I am looking forward to being able to give it to you. (I found it terribly difficult to let go of the last book — Fadensonnen — but you own it don't you?)[258]

My warmest greetings

Paul

124 [Stockholm] 11. 14. 1969

Paul, you dear one — what a joy for me to see your sparkling handwriting again. Thank you. I am at home again after I was in two different hospitals for almost about half a year, but I spend most of the time lying down. I have pains day and night and live for the hours when I take my pain-killers. I am so glad that you have a new apartment.

> Divide yourself night
> your two irradiated wings

tremble with horror
for I will go
and bring you back the bloody evening

Your Nelly

125 12. 15. 1969

Paul, dear You, many good wishes. All your poems are with me in this time of pain.

Your Nelly

126 [No date][259]

All gladness, dear Nelly, all light!

Eric, Gisèle, Paul

Editorial Afterword

For a period of almost 16 years — from early in 1954 until the end of 1969 — Nelly Sachs and Paul Celan exchanged letters with each other. The impressive completeness of the correspondence is evidence of the significance that both of them attached to it: one or two of Paul Celan's letters are missing from the beginning; at Celan's request Nelly Sachs partially destroyed a further letter from early in 1960; his telegrams from May and Summer 1960 are likewise no longer extant. Apart from these, however, both correspondents carefully preserved the letters of the other, Paul Celan even kept the envelopes (which helps to establish a few of the dates), his own drafts and carbon copies as well as documents relating to the only personal meetings in Spring and Fall 1960. The originals are now held at the Literaturarchiv in Marbach (Sachs) and in the Royal Library, Stockholm (Celan), to whom thanks are due for providing the sources.

Before the publication of this collection in the German edition in 1993, only a few of the letters between Nelly Sachs and Paul Celan were known. Her letters to Celan were not available to Ruth Dinesen and Helmut Müssener when they edited their selection of *Letters of Nelly Sachs.*[1] The few "Letters to Nelly Sachs" that appeared in 1988[2] and the comments on Celan's letters in Ruth Dinesen's Biography of Nelly Sachs[3] certainly convey something of the significance of the correspondence, but in these contexts it was especially clear that the interpretation of a letter depended upon knowledge of the letter to which it was responding, and that only a format encompassing the *exchange* of letters could do justice equally to both authors.

This is the first time the correspondence has been published in its entirety. Poems found with the letters have been included if they were integrated into a particular letter or were clearly intended as part of the epistolary conversation. Those found on the numerous supplementary folios — typescripts and off-prints — have not been included. It should be noted that the poems occasionally differ from their respective authorised printed versions — especially in the case of Nelly Sachs. Draft versions have only been included in their entirety if a final copy was lacking. The entries made by Paul Celan in his notebook during the meetings in Zurich and Paris have been included at appropriate points in the text; the few additional notes by Celan regarding Nelly Sachs have been incorporated into the notes.

References to place and date have been standardised (more detailed information on the address is given on the second line) and positioned before the text, sometimes with additional information derived from the context or from postmarks. Obvious writing errors have been corrected with due caution. Corrections of this kind have not been identified for the reader. The category "writing errors" does not include the characteristic linguistic peculiarities of the letters by Nelly Sachs; these should be seen as eloquent witnesses to her life and destiny. Among them are the influences of Swedish orthography ("internationelle Gallerien" [instead of "internationale Galerien"], "Salong" [instead of "Salon"]), words translated directly from the Swedish ("Preisausteilung" instead of "Preisverleihung" [prize-giving], "in innerster Bemerkung" instead of "im eigentlichen Sinn" [in the real or authentic sense]) and syntactical borrowings ("ich hatte Brief," "sobald sie erschien"). Her psychological state is also reflected in those passages where the syntax becomes confused, where fear "leaves her speechless." It is no coincidence that the problem of speechlessness is explicitly addressed in a sentence suffused with dread like the following (Letter 70): "The most terrible thing had happened to me and I can't find the words to say what in truth was behind the thing that brought me within a hair of mental and physical ruin." The absence of commas (commas are grammatically required in the German original — trans.) is a striking testimony to the dynamism of the distressed writer's need for self-expression, even if one considers the very reserved use of the comma that is characteristic of her poetry after 1958: Letter 50, for example, written on July 25, 1960 at the onset of a severe psychological crisis, is subdivided by a few periods but not by commas. For the addressee Paul Celan these linguistic peculiarities doubtless possessed semantic qualities. However, it was the wish of the literary heir that linguistic errors and punctuation should be judiciously corrected and/or added.

The endnotes provide factual explanations where these are necessary for a clear understanding of the letters and cross references to other passages within the correspondence. With the exception of very frequently-named persons such as Gudrun Dähnert and Celan's closest relatives Gisèle Celan-Lestrange and Eric Celan, who have been included in the index of persons under their family names, missing family names have consistently been added and unclear references to the titles of literary works have been made complete. Details on persons mentioned in the correspondence can be found in the index. Readers will also find information on specific circumstances relating to particular letters, such as enclosures and notes in a different hand, or references to draft versions — documents that testify to the care he took in writing to his correspondent.

The chronological table is focused mainly on the period covered by the correspondence. It was consciously intended to juxtapose the two lives in such a way that both the differences and the astonishing parallels will be apparent at one glance.

The annotated index of names covers all individuals mentioned in letters or in the notes. The index offers brief characterizations of the persons in question, insofar as this is relevant to the correspondence. The index does not, however, include authors of works translated by Sachs and Celan or of secondary literature cited in the notes.

Thanks are due to Hans Magnus Enzensberger and especially to Gisèle Celan-Lestrange, who did not live to see publication, for the kind permissions without which this edition could not have been produced. I owe thanks to Eric Celan for his kind permission to reproduce the etchings by his mother; thanks are also due to him and his collaborator Bertrand Badiou for their energetic assistance in the clarification of biographical questions, and to all those who were willing to provide information and thereby made a significant contribution to the project's success: Bernhard Böschenstein, Ruth Dinesen, Ute Doster (Deutsches Literaturarchiv Marbach), Kristina Eriksson (Royal Library Stockholm), Angelika Gundlach, Marieluise Hübscher-Bitter (Deutsche Akademie für Sprache und Dichtung), Christine Ivanovic, Henry Marx (Aufbau New York), Wolfgang Merz (Fischer Verlag), Nicolai Riedel (Deutsches Literaturarchiv Marbach), Ursula Sarrazin, Marita Wetzel (Deutsche Verlags-Anstalt).

Barbara Wiedemann
Regensburg, November 1992

Endnotes

[1] Frankfurt: Suhrkamp, 1984.

[2] in: Werner Hamacher, Winfried Menninghaus (eds.) *Paul Celan* (Frankfurt: Suhrkamp, 1988), pp. 14-19.

[3] Ruth Dinesen, *Nelly Sachs — Eine Biographie* (Frankfurt: Suhrkamp, 1992).

Editor's Notes to the Letters

Letter 1

[1] This first letter from Nelly Sachs is evidently preceded (see no. 96) by one or two letters from Celan that are no longer extant.
[2] *Mohn und Gedächtnis* [Poppy-seed and Memory]. In a letter to the Deutsche Verlags-Anstalt of 5.2.1954, Celan requested among other things that a copy be sent to Nelly Sachs.
[3] Seven poems appear in *Akzente* under the title "Beneath the Pole Star;" four of these are included in *Und Niemand weiß weiter* [And No-one knows the Way Onward].

Letter 2

[4] The journal *Botteghe Oscure* appeared in Rome bi-annually between 1949 and 1960 with contributions in Italian, French, German, Spanish and English. German contributions appeared in the Spring issues of each year. The imprint of the German section of 1958 and 1959 gives no indication that Celan and Bachmann were the editors.
[5] *Und Niemand weiß weiter*
[6] *In den Wohnungen des Todes* [In the Dwellings of Death], *Sternverdunkelung* [Eclipse of the Stars]

Letter 3

[7] Enclosed in this letter were the following poems, all of which subsequently appeared in *Botteghe Oscure* in the Spring of 1958: Siehe Daniel; Schon schmeckt die Zunge Sand im Brot; Und du riefst und riefst; Das Kind; Kein Wort birgt den magischen Kuß; Staubkörner rede ich; Röchelnde Umwege —; Ach daß man so wenig begreift.
[8] *Und Niemand weiß weiter*

Letter 4

[9] Cf. 3 n. 7
[10] *Und Niemand weiß weiter*
[11] Autumn issue 1957
[12] The Hebrew greeting means: Peace and blessing.

Letter 5

[13] The biographical notice in the Spring 1958 issue of *Botteghe Oscure* provides a very short summary of this list in English (see p. 541).
The bibliographical data contain several errors: *In den Wohnungen des Todes*; the subscription edition of *Eli, ein Mysterienspiel vom Leiden Israels* [Eli, a Mystery Play of the Suffering of Israel] did not appear until February 1951; *Aber auch*

diese Sonne ist heimatlos [This sun too is homeless] was published in Darmstadt (also with the Büchner Verlag).
[14] Nelly Sachs had been working on "Simson fällt durch Jahrtausende" in 1957.
[15] In 1961, scenes from *Eli* were read at an evening of recitations in the Landestheater in Darmstadt (where Sellner was Director) together with texts by Gertrud Kolmar and Else Lasker-Schüler.

Letter 7
[16] Nelly Sachs mistakenly writes 1957.
[17] "Eli, ein Mysterienspiel vom Leiden Israels," in the radio adaptation by Alfred Andersch, was broadcast for the first time by Norddeutscher Rundfunk on 21 May 1958.

Letter 9
[18] Nelly Sachs's letter appears on a typescript with the poems: Wer zuletzt hier stirbt; Jäger; In der Flucht; Im Alter; Heilige Minute; Tänzerin. In the printed version, the cycle contains 54 poems (not 40, as Nelly Sachs suggests here).

Letter 10
[19] The poem "Ein Auge, offen," which can be found in the Stockholm papers on a manuscript folio dated 28 May 1958, may have been enclosed with this letter.
[20] Eric Celan

Letter 11
[21] It is a long time before Nelly Sachs corrects the incorrect spelling of Gisèle Celan-Lestrange's name (see the question in the letter itself).
[22] Lenke Rothmann
[23] The etching by Gisèle Celan-Lestrange that was brought from Paris by Lenke Rothmann dates from 1956 and bears the title "Présence — Gegenwart" (25cm x 23cm, 25 copies printed); the print in question was an artist's copy dedicated by the artist herself with the words "pour Nelly Sachs."

Letter 12
[24] This is a mistake: Nelly Sachs had published with Bermann-Fischer, Aufbau and Ellermann; the first work she published with Deutsche Verlags-Anstalt was *Flucht und Verwandlung* [Flight and Metamorphosis]. She appears to have assumed that Celan would remain with the firm that had published his volume of poems *Von Schwelle zu Schwelle* [From Threshold to Threshold]. However, *Sprachgitter* [Bars of Language] appeared with Fischer Verlag (the contract was only signed on December 5/25, 1958).
[25] Eric Celan

Letter 13

[26] On the etching by Gisèle Celan-Lestrange, see no. 11.

[27] Nelly Sachs is alluding here to her deep disappointment over the musical version of *Eli* by Moses Pergament, which was broadcast on March 19, 1959 by Swedish Radio (Sveriges Radio, Stockholm).

[28] Nelly Sachs cites the last couplet from the poem "Hier ist kein Bleiben" from *Flucht und Verwandlung*.

Letter 14

[29] No date, postmark illegible. The meeting with Rudolf Peyer of which Nelly Sachs speaks appears to have taken place on 7.9.1959 (Letter to Peter Hamm of 7.9.1959: "Today I had a young friend of Paul Celan's here from Paris" in: *Briefe der Nelly Sachs*, p. 222).

[30] Rudolf Peyer adds a short greeting to the post-card.

[31] On the etching by Gisèle Celan-Lestrange, see no. 11.

Letter 15

[32] Rudolf Peyer, who is responsible for the first half of the post-card.

Letter 16

[33] Nelly Sachs compares Celan's volume of poems *Sprachgitter* with the "Zohar" ("Book of Radiance"), one of the most important works of the Kabbalah, the mystical occult doctrine of the Jews. For similar formulations, see letter to Peyer of 10.5.1959, *Briefe der Nelly Sachs*, p. 34 and the poem "Um Mitternacht:" "the mysteries of the Zohar / the magical book from Paris."

[34] This formulation draws on Nelly Sachs's own Zohar-poems in *Und Niemand weiß weiter*, particularly "Da schrieb der Schreiber des Zohar."

[35] The doctrine of the "tsimtsum" ("contraction," "limitation") dates back to the Jewish mystic Isaac Luria. Nelly Sachs may have encountered Lurian mysticism in Martin Buber's *Die chassidischen Bücher* (Berlin, 1927), or in Gerschom Scholem's work on Jewish mysticism, *Die jüdische Mystik in ihren Hauptströmungen* (Frankfurt, 1957) — the latter can still be found in her library; her formulations suggest that Scholem was the source (see Scholem, p. 287). The word "tsimtsum" denotes a concept that makes it possible to imagine a creation from nothing, without denying the omnipresence of God: namely the concept of God's voluntary withdrawal from a part of himself that he vacates to make way for the creation.

Letter 17

[36] Margarete Sachs

[37] Marguerite Caetani

[38] The Spring, 1958 edition of the journal *Botteghe Oscure*, Cf. 3/7

[39] A gift from Princess Caetani could no longer be found in the Stockholm bequest. The address that follows is presumably a Paris residence of the Princess.
[40] Poems by both of the authors named can be found in the Spring edition of 1960 (the last), the German-language section of which was edited by Hans Magnus Enzensberger.
[41] On the etching by Gisèle Celan-Lestrange, see no. 11.
[42] Eric Celan

Letter 18
[43] The review of *Sprachgitter* by Günter Blöcker appeared in the Berlin *Tagesspiegel* of 10.11.1959, Nr 4283, p. 39. Nelly Sachs did not preserve the items enclosed with this letter. Blöcker's review is directed against what he takes to be the insufficient sense of reality in *Sprachgitter*, a characteristic that he explains through a reference to Celan's origins. Celan understood this to be a reference to his "Jewish origins." (Blöcker:) "Celan handles the German language with greater freedom than most of his fellow poets. That may be because of his background. The communicative character of the language limits and weighs him down less than it does others. Though it must be said that this means he often succumbs to the temptation to operate in a void."

Letter 19
[44] Nelly Sachs is presumably referring to the very painful ending of her relationship with Peter Hamm
[45] Günter Blöcker, Cf. 18 and 21
[46] Peter Hamm, Cf. 14/29
[47] One year later, Paul Celan will write "The Meridian" above the text of his Büchner speech.

Letter 20
[48] The extant letter from Günter Blöcker does not make it clear who is being referred to here.
[49] Peter Hamm, Cf. 21/50

Letter 21
[50] Günter Blöcker, *Die neuen Wirklichkeiten. Linien und Profile der modernen Literatur* (Berlin, 1957) [Engl.: The New Realities. Lines and Profiles in Modern Literature]. The book deals generally with twentieth-century authors. Paul Celan is not mentioned.

Letter 22
[51] Celan's translation, Osip Mandelstam, *Gedichte*, appeared in the Fall of 1959.

[52] Despite the apparent concreteness of the announcement, this project was not completed in 1960.
[53] Enclosed with the letter was a typescript with the following poems: Geist; Der Schwan; Wer / von der Erde kommt; Im Gewitter.

Letter 23
[54] The reference is to the translation of Paul Valéry, *La jeune Parque* [The Young Fate], in an edition comprising verses 1-173.

Letter 26
[55] First publication in: "Briefe an Nelly Sachs," p. 14.
[56] Eric Celan
[57] It is not clear to whom Celan is referring.

Letter 28
[58] Celan's completed translation of Paul Valéry, *La jeune Parque*
[59] Translation from Celan's rendering in German of Valéry's "chargés de jour et de créations" (GW IV, p. 160/61)
[60] The photograph taken by Anna Riwkin bears a dedication on the verso: "For my friends / Paul and Giselle Celan // in the moment of existence / listening deeply to each other // Nelly Sachs / Stockholm, 3.24.60."
[61] Cf. 11
[62] Dresden is the home of Gudrun Dähnert.

Letter 29
[63] Eva-Lisa Lennartsson
[64] The reason for the journey was the award of the Meersburg Prize for Women Poets. It was conferred for the second time on May 29, 1960.
[65] Nelly Sachs had been invited to join Alfred Andersch in the Tessin region of Switzerland.

Letter 31
[66] Nelly Sachs's fear of persecution in the early months of 1960 had a realistic foundation in the increased circulation of anti-Semitic literature at that time. The Swedish government took action in February (see Ruth Dinesen, *Nelly Sachs. Eine Biographie*, Frankfurt, 1992, p. 301). See also the letters to Moses and Ilse Pergament and Rudolf Peyer (*Briefe der Nelly Sachs*, nos. 158, 160 amd 161).
[67] Cf. 29/65

Letter 32
[68] The relevant issue of *Documents* appeared in 1953 with translations by Gilbert Socard; the 1953 issue printed "Chor der Schatten" and the two poems men-

tioned in the letter.

[69] This is Celan's rendering; in *Documents* and *In den Wohnungen des Todes*, however, the word is "they" ("sie").

[70] In the form in which it has been preserved, the letter carries no signature and is certainly not complete. This impression is strengthened by a draft letter dated the previous day that survives in the Celan papers. It would appear that parts of this letter have been incorporated — in a milder form — into the letter that was sent. In view of the nature of the accusations levelled against Alfred Andersch, it is likely that this is the part of the letter that Celan asked Nelly Sachs to destroy. She reports on its destruction in Letter 44. Claire Goll had just published her accusations of plagiarism in the May issue of *Baubudenpoet*, and this too may have been mentioned in the destroyed section of the letter (Cf. the answering letter no. 34). The charges levelled against Andersch cannot be proven, they are presumably reactions to hearsay information; this is doubtless also the means by which Celan learnt that Nelly Sachs had been invited to visit Alfred Andersch.

"Dear, good Nelly Sachs,

You once wrote to me that the meridian of pain runs between Stockholm and Paris.
I am going to have speak to you of painful things, dear Nelly Sachs, almost *daily* I am overwhelmed by the infamy of people. And hardly one that stands by me. It serves me right, they think.

I am going to have to name the names of the base ones; the name Alfred Andersch is one of them.
I can do no other, dear Nelly Sachs, I must say this to you. I am telling the truth.

From my heart
Your Paul Celan

I wrote these lines this morning — then I hesitated to send them to you. No, I will send them to you after all, Nelly Sachs. I can't conceal from you what is true, true in itself, and true a second time by virtue of the tears we have wept here.
This Andersch *is* a villain, and the praise that he lavishes upon you is a villain's praise. For this too, Nelly Sachs, is true: that the "promotion" of your poems by this man came precisely at a time when your poems were already on their way, on those invisible paths that poetry walks, led by a quiet hand. Do please travel to Switzerland. But *please*, don't be deceived! Don't let them lie to you dear Nelly Sachs!"

Letter 33
[71] Cf. 29/64
[72] Cf. 29/65
[73] Cf. 31/66

Letter 34
[74] Cf. 32/70
[75] Cf. 31/66
[76] The German original is a literal translation of the Swedish "i innersta bemärkelse," for "in the real sense."
[77] This is presumably a reference to the invitation to visit Alfred Andersch in Tessin.
[78] Alfred Andersch was in Stockholm for a reading in March.
[79] Eva-Lisa Lennartsson
[80] Ivan Goll
[81] This publication in *Aufbau*, a German-language Jewish weekly in New York can no longer be found. Nor is there a copy in the Stockholm papers.
[82] Claire Goll's role in the editing of *Aufbau* can no longer be established. She may have been engaged as an occasional freelance employee.
[83] Gudrun Dähnert

Letter 35
[84] Cf. Letter no. 32/70
[85] Cf. 34/81,82
[86] Manfred George

Letter 36
[87] Kurt Juster
[88] Cf. 34/81,82
[89] Claire Goll
[90] Ivan Goll

Letter 37
[91] She is replying to a request by telegram from Paul Celan. In his note book there is an entry under the date May 15: "Nelly Sachs Telegram: she shouldn't speak with anyone." The telegram is no longer extant.
[92] Cf. 31/66
[93] The meeting between Nelly Sachs and Paul Celan did indeed take place in the Hotel zum Storchen in Zurich, Cf. Celan's following letter with "Zürich, Zum Storchen," which is dedicated to Nelly Sachs.
[94] Nelly Sachs is thinking of Rembrandt's painting of 1656, "Jacob's Blessing," that depicts the blessing of Joseph's two sons Ephraim and Manasseh.

According to Genesis 48 Jacob blesses Ephraim as the first-born, although he is the younger and explicitly defends this decision to their father. In Rembrandt's very sombre painting the blessing "blooms" as a bright glow. Nelly Sachs owned the brief treatise by Herbert von Einem *Der Segen Jakobs von Rembrandt van Rijn* (Berlin, 1948); on this see also her poem "Lange."

Letter 38
[95] Ingeborg Bachmann
[96] Restaurant in Zurich
[97] Celan quotes the word "Beschäftigter" (one who is busy, occupied) in the masculine form, in accordance with Nelly Sachs' verbal assurance that the "Du" (you) in the poem referred to Celan himself. But in the manuscript left with him by Nelly Sachs, the word appears as "Beschäftigte" (the female form, or possibly an error).
[98] Nelly Sachs travelled to Meersburg by train and ship, Paul Celan did not attend the awarding of the prize.

Letter 40
[99] [Translator's note:] Paul Celan uses the intimate form "Du" in this poem, and this is the form of address employed throughout the rest of the correspondence. In this context the opening strophe of the poem can be seen as an allusion to the meeting between Celan and Sachs in Zurich, in the course of which Nelly Sachs as the older of the two friends proposed that they address each other with "Du" (see the notes relating to Wednesday in no. 38).
[100] The date is written in the hand of Gudrun Dähnert, whose text precedes that of Nelly Sachs. Her detailed letter expressly thanks Celan for his poem (no. 39) and also describes the celebrations in Meersburg.
[101] Eric Celan
[102] Celan's whole family had picked up Nelly Sachs from Zurich airport, Cf. "selbdritt" (the three of us) in no. 38.
[103] Nelly Sachs mistakenly writes *July*.

Letter 41
[104] Nelly Sachs came to Paris with her friend Eva-Lisa Lennartson, who had already accompanied her to Meersburg and into Tessin and adds a greeting to the letter.

Letter 42
[105] Celan mistakenly writes *July*.
[106] June 13, the day on which Nelly Sachs arrives in Paris, is a Monday.
[107] Martha-Hotel, 97 Rue Lauriston, Paris 16e.
[108] Eva-Lisa Lennartson

Letter 43

[109] Paul Celan led Nelly Sachs to important tourist sites of the inner city of Paris: to the churches of St Julien, St Séverin and the Ste Chappelle, into the Latin Quarter, the Jardin du Luxembourg, to Montmartre with the Place du Tertre (where the painters stand) and the grave of Heinrich Heine in Montmartre Cemetery, into the Marais Quarter with the Place des Vosges and the Musée Carnavalet (an historic museum of the city), and finally to the café formerly famous as a meeting place for intellectuals, "Aux Deux Magots" on the Boulevard St. Germain.

[110] École Normale Supérieure, Celan's place of work.

[112] "Infamy" is the word Celan uses to describe the defamations that followed the accusations by Claire Goll.

[112] The reference is to "Du / in der Nacht," Cf. 38/97.

[113] Margarete Sachs

Letter 44

[114] Cf. the poem "Einer steht" in her following letter (no. 46).

[115] Gisèle Celan-Lestrange left a greeting with best wishes for Nelly Sachs in the hotel.

[116] In the Stockholm papers there is a photograph of Paul Celan taken by Gisèle Celan-Lestrange, inscribed on the back with following words in Paul Celan's hand: "Paris, 78 rue de Longchamp, 1958."

[117] No works by Martin Buber with dedications by Paul Celan could be found among the Stockholm papers. It not clear which two books are meant and whether they were presented to her personally by Paul Celan or sent to her by post. (Translator's note: Professor Otto Pöggeler reports that Celan sent two phonograph records of Buber reading, not two books. I am grateful to Professor John Felstiner of Stanford University for drawing this to my attention.)

[118] This refers to the destruction of part of a letter to which Nelly Sachs replied in her letters no. 34 and 35.

Letter 45

[119] First publication in: "Briefe an Nelly Sachs," pp. 14f.

[120] Nelly Sachs sent a copy of *Flucht and Verwandlung* from Stockholm. In her dedication she refers to the motto and poem: "In der Flucht:" "In place of a homeland / I have / Paul/ Gisèle / Eric // To my sister-soul Gisèle / with love and thanks! / Nelly / Stockholm / on June 18, 1960 / one day after the departure —."

[121] Cf. the end of the poem "Zu beiden Händen," also written on 7.1.1960: The Same / has lost / us, the / Same / has forgotten / us, the / Same / has — us"

[122] An edition of *Die Judenbuche* by Annette von Droste-Hülshoff can no longer be found in the Stockholm library; nor was it possible to identify bibliographi-

cally the edition referred to here. Celan may be referring to a publication of the Galerie Flechtheim owned by the art publisher Alfred Flechtheim.

[123] The envelope from Werner Weber's letter with the post-mark dated 6.30.1960 is still in the correspondence; on it can be the found the following words in Celan's handwriting (with a mistaken reference to the month): "Letter forwarded to Nelly Sachs 6.1.1960." Nelly Sachs sent "Mund /saugend am Tod" (Mouth / suckling at death) (Cf. no. 47). The *Neue Zürcher Zeitung*, of which Weber was the cultural affairs editor, published it together with Celan's poem "Zürich, Zum Storchen" (Zurich, the Stork Hotel) and a note on the first meeting of the two poets on 8.7.1960.

Letter 47

[124] Refers to the poem "Einer steht" in Letter no. 46.

[125] A typescript of "Mund / saugend am Tod" was enclosed with the letter.

[126] The house in which Nelly Sachs lived was owned by the Jewish community of Stockholm. The planned exchange of apartments never took place.

Letter 48

[127] First published in: "Briefe an Nelly Sachs," p. 15f. There are two extant draft versions of this letter.

[128] Also signed with the words: "Avec Eric et de tout cœur / Gisèle."

Letter 49

[129] Although it contains no reference to the postal date, this telegram has been placed here on account of the fact that it was forwarded, like Letter no. 50 of July 25, 1960, from Kermovan to Paris. Inge Waern had informed Celan by letter and by telephone of Nelly Sachs's critical condition and had also conveyed her wish to see him in Stockholm. The telegram from Celan that presumably preceded this one is no longer extant.

Letter 50

[130] Neo-fascist groups were indeed active in Stockholm at this time (Cf. "Briefe an Nelly Sachs," no. 161). It was not possible to discover whether a group bearing this name was among them. Cf. 31/66

[131] The correspondence with the Office for Compensation [Entschädigungsamt] in Berlin can still be found in the Stockholm papers. The procedure referred to here was only completed on April 25, 1961, with the decision to grant Nelly Sachs DM 20,000 in compensation for the confiscation of the house of Margarete Sachs in Lessingstraße, Berlin.

[132] A handwritten alteration to the will is still extant. An accompanying note permits it to be dated to July 26, 1960. On December 5, 1960, this alteration was formally certified by Nelly Sachs's attorney, Julius Hepner. In its present

form, the letter bears no signature. As her postal address Nelly Sachs gives the address of Hella Appeltoft.

Letter 51

[133] First published in "Briefe an Nelly Sachs," pp. 16f.

[134] Eric Celan's glass window survives among the papers. The text is followed by the words "Alles, alles Gute! Gisèle"

Letter 52

[135] Astrid Ivarsson

[136] At first, Nelly Sachs lived at the home of Inge Waerne.

[137] Refers to unknown plans for travel that may be connected with a telephone call by Celan to Nelly Sachs.

Letter 54

[138] First published in "Briefe an Nelly Sachs," p. 17.

Letter 55

[139] Cf. Celan's translation of Sergei Esenin, *Gedichte* [Poems].

Letter 56

[140] Celan's letter (no. 55) is written on two post-cards.

[141] Gudrun Dähnert added a few lines to the letter.

Letter 57

[142] First published in "Briefe an Nelly Sachs," pp. 17f.

[143] Also signed "Eric" and "Yours in deepest heartfelt gratitude, Gisèle."

Letter 58

[144] Gudrun Dähnert added a postscript to the letter.

Letter 59

[145] The telegram is no longer extant.

Letter 61

[146] Daniel Brick, editor of *Judisk Krönika.*

[147] Both Gudrun Dähnert and Anna Riwkin added their greetings to the letter.

Letter 62

[148] In the upper right corner of the telegram, Celan noted the text of his reply: "Can be with you on the fourth warmest P. — " He appears to have made an error regarding the date (27th). The telegram itself does not survive.

[149] The Stockholm hospital where Nelly Sachs was being treated at this time.

Letter 63
[150] Julius Hepner
[151] Cf. 62/149

Letter 64
[152] In the upper right corner of the telegram, Gisèle Celan-Lestrange has noted the time of arrival: 11.30. A draft version of the return telegram written in her hand with the annotation "31 août midi" survives among the papers: "Paul has not booked a room will be with you tomorrow early in the morning." Celan had already left Paris by train from the Gare du Nord on August 30 and arrived in Stockholm on September 1. The tickets were filed with the correspondence.
[153] The Sankt-Eriks-Mäsan, is an annual Fall trade fair that has taken place in Stockholm since 1943.

Letter 65
[154] In the upper right corner of the telegram, Gisèle Celan-Lestrange has noted the time of arrival: "18 heures."
[155] Cf. 62/149

Letter 66
[156] The psychiatric clinic in which Nelly Sachs received further treatment after her emergency admission to the Södersjukhus.
[157] This is a reference to Israel ben Elieser, known as Baal Shem Tov, the founder of Hasidism. See also the poems "Eine Schöpfungsminute im Auge des Baalschem" and "Auf der äußersten Spitze der Landzunge," both from a group of poems enclosed with letters 68 (11.24.1960) and 69 (12.5.1960). Nelly Sachs also projected the Baal Shem figure onto to the person of Paul Celan, as for example in a typescript version of the scene "Was ist ein Opfer?" [What is a sacrifice?]: "For Paul Celan / For the poet of the unsayable / the Baal Shem-man who keeps the balance / for the friend of the lonely / Nelly Sachs / April 23, 1960."

Letter 67
[158] This letter also survives in a draft version.

Letter 68
[159] Dr Sten Mårtens.
[160] Cf. 66/156
[161] Literal translation of the Swedish "Prisutdelning"; she is referring to the award of the Büchner Prize to Celan in Darmstadt on 10.22.1960.

Letter 70

[162] Gunnar Josephson as head of the Jewish community (Mosaiska Församlingen)

[163] The certification of this change to Nelly Sachs's will is dated 12.5.1960, the day on which this letter was written. Cf. 50/132.

[164] Cf. 62/149.

[165] Margarete Sachs

[166] Cf. 50/131.

[167] The following poems from the cycle "Noch feiert Tod das Leben" [Death Still Celebrates the Life] are enclosed with the letter: Der versteinerte Engel, Wunder der Begegnungen, Hinter der Tür.

[168] Cf. 66/156.

Letter 72

[169] Cf. the items enclosed with nos. 70 and 71 and the two poems sent on 12.14.1960.

[170] Sergei Esenin, *Gedichte* appeared in March 1961.

[171] "Der Meridian" did not appear until March 1961.

Letter 74

[172] The convalescent home mentioned in letter 69.

[173] Nelly Sachs uses the Swedish word for boarding-house [Pensionat].

Letter 75

[174] Cf. 74. In Paul Celan's notebook there is a reference to this letter in the handwriting of Gisèle Celan-Lestrange: "Lettre de Nelly Sachs qui nous invite en Suède, envoie un poème, mais ne dit rien de cette sordide horreur dont elle a sûrement connaissance. Elle a un poème dans le même numéro de / / où il y a la prise de position de / /. Elle évite le sujet." [Letter from Nelly Sachs, who invites us to Sweden, sends a poem, but says nothing of this sordid horror that she must be aware of. She has a poem in the same issue of / / where / /'s view is expressed. She avoids the subject." The identity of the publication and person denoted by the areas (/ /) of subsequently erased text cannot be established with certainty. But they doubtless refer to a response to the accusations made by Claire Goll.

[175] Berta Antschel, the sister of Leo Antschel.

[176] Odette Lestrange.

[177] Inge Waern, Eva-Lisa Lennartson.

Letter 76

[178] Cf. 66/156.

[179] Hans Magnus Enzensberger adds a few sentences of greetings to the letter.

Letter 78

[180] Engl: "Be healthy!"

Letter 79

[181] Gudrun Dähnert adds a letter of her own to this letter, in the course of which she recalls Paul Celan's visit to Stockholm at the beginning of September 1960 with the words: "One of her first words to me was that she was so infinitely pained by the fact that she had failed to recognize her best friends and you above all, to whom she feels so close. And I told her how saddened you had been when you left."

Letter 81

[183] This is a draft version marked with the words: "Not sent."

Letter 82

[183] Since Celan's previous letter (no. 78) only one poem had been sent by Nelly Sachs that can still be found in the correspondence. It is "Wer ruft," which was enclosed with letter 80.

[184] Sergei Esenin, *Gedichte.*

[185] Early Celan translations of Esenin can be found in the papers of Alfred Margul-Sperber in the Museum of Literature, Bucarest.

Letter 83

[186] Cf. 74/173

[187] Sergei Esenin, *Gedichte.*

[188] The sequence of tenses employed here is borrowed from the Swedish.

Letter 85

[189] The year is noted on the envelope by an unidentifiable hand; the post-mark is illegible.

[190] A reference to the staff of Beckomberga Sjukhus, Cf. 66/156.

Letter 86

[191] This letter survives only in the form of a carbon-copy in the Celan papers.

[192] Presumably a reference to "Weiß im Krankenhauspark" [White in the Hospital Park] (letter 85), which was published for the first time in March.

[193] Postscript by Gisèle Celan-Lestrange: "All best wishes, dear Nelly / Warm greetings, Your Gisèle."

Letter 87

[194] This is a reference to a conversation between Nelly Sachs and Paul Celan on

Ascension Day 1960 in Zurich and a quotation from Celan's poem "Zurich, the Stork Hotel."

Letter 88
[195] Nelly Sachs was referring to Beckomberga Hospital, Cf. 66/156.
[196] A short post-script by Gudrun Dähnert follows.

Letter 89
[197] This is a reference to their first meeting, on the occasion of the Droste Prize Award at the end of May, 1960.
[198] Nelly Sachs visited the Celan family in Paris from June 13 to 17, 1960.
[199] This refers to Celan's journey of September 1-7, 1960 to Stockholm where he visited the sick Nelly Sachs.
[200] Signature follows: "Gisèle"

Letter 90
[201] Gunnar Ekelöf and Erik Lindegren, *Weil unser einziges Nest unsere Flügel sind.*
[202] Presumably a reference to the etching given in 1958 (Cf. letter 11).

Letter 95
[203] On 8.5.1964, Celan had sent an offprint with his translation of William Shakespeare, "Eighteen Sonnets."
[204] Dr Sten Mårtens.

Letter 96
[205] A comprehensive draft version of this letter, dating from the previous day, is also extant.
[206] *Glühende Rätsel* (1964).
[207] The draft version gives a somewhat more precise account of the chronology: "Ten years ago, or, more precisely, ten-and-a-half years ago, I had written to you after reading *Wohnungen* to ask if you could let me have a copy of *Sternverdunkelung.* Then we exchanged letters, not a few of them, then you came, then you fell ill, then I came because you had called me to you in Stockholm."

Letter 98
[208] On October 20, 1966, the Nobel Prize Committee announced its decision to award the Nobel Prize for Literature to Nelly Sachs and Josef S. Agnon.

Letter 99
[209] The Nobel Prize award ceremony took place in Stockholm on this day; it coincided with the 75th birthday of Nelly Sachs.

Letter 100

[210] Included among the materials filed with the correspondence is a list of the poems selected to be read. Celan read (or planned to read) the following poems: From the collection *Fahrt ins Staublose*: Chor der Steine, Chor der Ungeborenen, Greise, Da du / unter dem Fuß dir, Ein Schwarzer Jochanaan, Bereit sind, Hier unten, In der Flucht, Zwischen, Im Alter, Mutter, Du / in der nacht, Überall Jerusalem, Diese Kette; from the series "Glühende Rätsel," i.e. from the collected volume *Späte Gedichte* of 1966: Diese Nacht, Weine aus, Im verhexten Wald, Immer wieder, Gesichte aus Dämmerung, Steine trugst Du, Hölle, Bin in der Fremde..., Sie stießen zusammen, Schneller Zeit; from *Die Suchende*: Du bist der Weissager der Sterne.

Letter 101

[211] This letter accompanied a folio entitled "Scraps of Sleep, Wedges," an etching by Gisèle Celan-Lestrange with the poem by Paul Celan.

[212] Signed also: "Eric" and "Gisèle."

Letter 102

[213] This presumably refers to the tape recording of the event held in honor of Nelly Sachs at the Paris Goethe-Institute (Cf. letter 100). Since March 1992, the tape has been deposited with the Stockholm papers.

[214] Bengt Holmqvist, *Den moderna litteraturen* (Stockholm, 1966); a German edition was never published.

Letter 103

[215] [Translator's note] Bavarian-Austrian dial.: a tumbler for wine or schnaps

[216] [Translator's note] "Kakanien" (Engl.: Kakania), a play on the initials K & K (kaiserlich & königlich; Engl.: imperial and royal), was the name used by Robert Musil for the fictional Austro-Hungarian landscape of his novel *The Man without Qualities.*

[217] [Translator's note] Latin for "we have seen" (German orig.: Vidimierung): certification, mark appended to a document indicating its authenticity.

[218] Also signed: "Gisèle" and "Bengt."

Letter 104

[219] This presumably refers to the volume *Atemwende*, which was released at the end of August.

[220] This is a reference to *Die Suchende.*

[221] Cf. "Zurich, The Stork Hotel" and nos. 38 and 57.

[222] *Atemkristall.*

Letter 105
[223] First published in "Briefe an Nelly Sachs," p. 18.
[224] Cf. 108/228.
[225] From this point onwards, Celan gives his place of work (École Normale Supérieure, 45 rue d'Ulm) as his personal address.

Letter 106
[226] The greeting is written on the back of a post-card with a reproduction of Marc Chagall's "Le marchand des bestiaux," 1912, Kunstmuseum Basel.

Letter 108
[227] First published in "Briefe an Nelly Sachs," p. 19.
[228] See also the poem "Nah, im Aortabogen" in *Fadensonnen*: "Ziv, that light."

Letter 109
[229] Cf. 28/60,61.
[230] Gisèle Celan-Lestrange's work had been seen at solo-exhibitions in Wuppertal and Bremen (1958), in Hanover (1964), in the Paris Goethe-Institute (1966), and in Bochum (1967). In 1968 she exhibited in Stuttgart, Bielefeld, Frankfurt and Freiburg, as well as Göteborg.
[231] As a member of the artists' group "Graveurs de Paris."

Letter 112
[232] In 1968, Dr Sten Mårtens, her doctor in Beckomberga, took up the post of head physician at Rålambshov hospital.
[233] Contrary to Nelly Sachs's belief, Gisèle Celan-Lestrange was not in Göteborg at the time of her exhibition there. In a letter of 5.11.1968, she writes to Nelly Sachs: "It wasn't possible to travel there, because I am working here as a teacher."

Letter 113
[234] This refers to an etching made in March 1968: "Nos frères — Unsere Brüder" [Engl.: Our brothers].
[235] The invitation was sent on 4.4.1968 with a short letter.
[236] Eva-Lisa Lennartsson
[237] Lenke Rothmann
[238] Jules Supervielle, *Gedichte*

Letter 114
[239] Nelly Sachs mistakenly writes 4.2.1968.
[240] Cf. 112/233.
[241] Toby Brandt

[242] The art critic could not be identified.
[243] Dr. Sten Mårtens

Letter 115
[244] Celan wrote on the back on the envelope: "recvd: 6.15.68. Two days before: The N. Sachs-Book" (i.e. *Das Buch der Nelly Sachs*). The late arrival is presumably due to the widespread unrest in Paris during May 1968; Paris was occasionally cut off from all postal traffic.
[245] Nelly Sachs evidently assumed that the negotiations with a Stockholm Gallery to take over the Göteborg exhibition had been successfully completed. But no exhibition of works by Gisèle Celan-Lestrange took place in Stockholm.
[246] Dr Sten Mårtens

Letter 118
[247] Since the autumn issue of 1968 (No. 7), Paul Celan had been co-editor of *L'Éphémère* with Yves Bonnesfoy, André du Bouchet, Jacques Dupin, Louis-René des Forêts, and Gaëtan Picon.
[248] Celan knew Lortholary personally as a student at the École Normale Supérieure. He was doubtless thinking of the translations: Chœur de ceux qu'on a sauvés (Chorus of the Saved), Tous les Pays sont prêts (Every Land is Ready), Dans la Fuite (In Flight), Ce collier d'énigmes (This Chain of Riddles).
[249] Under the date 2.10.1969, Nelly Sachs writes on the letter: "sent 'Dream that [overgrows] the Sleeper'," Cf. letter 119.

Letter 119
[250] *Die Suchende*
[251] Cf. letter 50.
[252] "Dream that Overgrows the Sleeper" [Traum der den Schlafenden überwächst]

Letter 120
[253] The poem "Traum der den Schlafenden überwächst" appeared together with Bernard Lortholary's translation, "Rêve surcroît du dormeur" in "L'Éphémère," no. 9, 1969.

Letter 121
[254] Cf. 120/253.

Letter 122
[255] This is written on a post-card showing the Damascus Gate in Jerusalem.

Letter 123

[256] While in Tel-Aviv, Celan gave his "Address to the Hebrew Writers' Association."

[257] *Lichtzwang* in fact appeared on June 2, 1970.

[258] There is no trace of this volume in the Stockholm library.

Letter 126

[259] The date of this letter could not be established. It is presumably a New Year's greeting, which could have been placed elsewhere in the correspondence. However, the fact that Eric Celan and Gisèle Celan-Lestrange have not signed the letter suggest that this letter was written relatively late.

Annotated Index of Names

Agnon (Czaczkes), Josef Samuel (1888-1970)
A Galician-born author, mainly of narrative prose works, first in Yiddish, later in Hebrew. In 1966 he received the Nobel Prize for Literature together with Nelly Sachs.
Letter 98.

Allemann, Beda (1926-1991)
Professor of German Literature, first at the University of Würzburg, then from 1967 until his death in Bonn. Paul Celan appointed him literary executor of his estate and he took charge of the historical-critical edition of Celan's works, of which, however, he was only able to complete the volume *Atemwende*. Editor of: *Ausgewählte Gedichte* (1968), *Gedichte in zwei Bänden* (1975), *Gesammelte Werke in fünf Bänden* (together with Stefan Reichert, assisted by Rolf Bücher, 1983).
Letter 100

Andersch, Alfred (1914-1980)
German writer resident in Switzerland from 1958. Editor of the journal *Texte und Zeichen*, in which both Nelly Sachs and Paul Celan had works published. As a broadcasting editor he promoted works by Nelly Sachs, including the radio version of "Eli". Nelly Sachs was in contact with him from 1956 onwards and visited him in the Tessin region of Switzerland in 1960.
Letters 7, 29, 32, 34

Antschel, Berta (1894-1981)
Sister of Leo Antschel. She lived in London, where Paul Celan occasionally visited her.
Letters 75, 109

Antschel, Leo (1890-1942?)
Father of Paul Celan, died in the Michailowka camp (Ukraine). [Translator's note: In his introduction to *Paul Celan. Selected Poems* (Penguin: Harmondsworth, 1988), Michael Hamburger states (p. 19) that Paul Celan's father died of typhus. His mother was killed by a shot in the back of the neck.]
Letter 75

Appeltoft, Hella
Friend of Nelly Sachs in Stockholm
Letter 50

Bachmann, Ingeborg (1926-1973)
Austrian author whom Paul Celan knew from the short time he had spent in Vienna (1948). She met Nelly Sachs for the first time during her stay in Zurich and Meersburg in 1960.
Letters 2, 31, 34, 38

Blöcker, Günter (b. 1913)
Journalist and author, regular freelance writer with numerous radio stations, journals and newspapers. Author of a review of *Sprachgitter* that Celan found deeply hurtful: "Gedichte als graphische Gebilde," *Tagespiegel*, Berlin, 10.11.1959.
Letters 18, 19, 20, 21

Bonnefoy, Yves (b. 1923)
French poet, co-founder and co-editor of the journal *L'Éphémère* (Paris).
Letter *118*

Bouchet, André du (b. 1924)
French poet, co-editor of the journal *L'Éphémère* (Paris). He translated a number of Celan's poems; Celan also translated a number of Bouchet's poems in *Vakante Glut* (1968).
Letter *118*

Brick, Daniel (b. 1903)
Journalist with *Judisk Krönika*, a Jewish journal in Sweden. Married to Anna Riwkin.
Letter 65

Brandt, Emmy, née Sachs
Paternal cousin of Nelly Sachs
Letter 114

Brandt, Toby
Married to Emmy Brandt
Letter 114

Buber, Martin (1878-1965)
German-Jewish philosopher and writer who attempted to make Hasidism accessible to a contemporary readership. Nelly Sachs devoted intense study to his work.
Letters *16*, 44

Caetani, Marguerite, née Chapin
During the inter-war period she published the journal *Commerce* in Paris, after the war in Rome she published the international literary journal *Botteghe Oscure* (1949-1960), in which both Nelly Sachs (1958, 1959, 1960) and Paul Celan (1956,1958) had works published, on the suggestion of her assistant, Stanley Moss, in 1957. She was a princess by virtue of her marriage to pianist Roffredo Caetani.
Letters 2, 3, 4, 17

Celan, Eric (b. 1955)
Son of Gisèle Celan-Lestrange and Paul Celan
Letters 10, 12, 17, 26, 40, 44, 45, 47, 48, 50, 51, 52, 53, 55, 56, 57, 58, 61, 63, 66, 67, 68, 69, 72, 74, 75, 76, 79, 82, 84, 85, 87, 88, 90, 93, 94, 96, 97, 100, *101*, 102, 104, 126

Celan-Lestrange, Gisèle, née de Lestrange (1927-1991)
French graphic artist married to Paul Celan from 1952. Her pictures were shown in solo exhibitions in her home city of Paris and in many other European cities, including Göteborg (Sweden). Work in collaboration with Paul Celan (including *Atemkristall, Schwarzmaut*), who is responsible for the bilingual titles of her works until 1970.
Letters 11, 12, 13, 14, 17, 28, 34, 40, 43, 44, 45, 47, *48*, *51*, 52, 53, 56, 57, 58, 61, 63, 64, 65, 66, 67, 68, 69, 71, 73, 74, 75, 76, 77, 79, 82, 84, 85, *86*, 87, 88, 89, 90, 93, 94, 96, 97, 98, 99, 100, *101*, 102, *103*, 104, 109, 110, 111, 112, 113, 114, 115, 126

Chagall, Marc (1887-1985)
Letter 106

Dähnert, Gudrun, née Harlan (1907-1976)
Closest friend of Nelly Sachs until her death. She used a journey to Sweden in 1939 to prepare the way for entry into Sweden of Nelly Sachs and her mother. Travelled from her home in Dresden (GDR) to visit Nelly Sachs on a number of occasions after the war.
Letters 17, 28, 33, 34, 40, 50, 52, 53, 55, 56, 57, 58, 61, 68, 70, 79, *88*, 89, 103

Droste-Hülshoff, Annette von (1797-1848)
Letter 45

Dupin, Jacques (b. 1927)
French poet, co-editor of the journal *L'Éphémère* (Paris). Celan translated his cycle of poems "La nuit grandissante" ("Die Nacht, größer und größer," 1970).
Letter *118*

Edfelt, Johannes (b. 1904)
Swedish poet and literary critic, the first person to promote and translate the poems of Nelly Sachs in Sweden; Sachs also translated poems by Edfelt (*Der Schattenfischer*, 1958). Author of numerous reviews of Celan and other contemporary German authors.
Letter 3

Ellermann, Heinrich (1905-1991)
Publisher of a volume of poems by Nelly Sachs (*Und Niemand weiß weiter*).
Letter 5

Enzensberger, Hans Magnus (b. 1929)
Close and friendly contact with Nelly Sachs after 1958, when Enzensberger lived in Norway for a short time (1957-1958, 1961). He edited her work as *Lektor* for Suhrkamp Verlag and was her legal heir.
Letters 7, *17*, 43, 76

Flechtheim, Alfred (1878-1937)
Art publisher and gallery owner, editor of the journal *Der Querschnitt* (Münster).
Letter 45

Forêts, Louis René des (b. 1918)
French novelist and poet, co-editor of the journal *L'Éphémère* (Paris).
Letter *118*

George, Manfred (1893-1965)
Cousin of Nelly Sachs. After his emigration to the United States he was publisher and editor-in-chief (from 1939) of the German-Jewish weekly newspaper *Aufbau* (New York).
Letters 34, 35

Goll, Claire, née Klara Aischmann (1890-1977)
As the wife of Yvan Goll, she was in contact with Paul Celan from his early years in Paris. In 1960 she stirred up a defamation campaign against Paul Celan when she published an article in the journal *Baubudenpoet* (Munich, no. 5, pp. 115f: "Unbekanntes über Paul Celan") in which she accused him of having plagiarized the work of her husband.

Goll, Yvan (=Isaac Lang) (1891-1950)
Poet in the German and the French language. Paul Celan was in contact with him after his departure from Vienna and translated (unpublished) the volumes

of his poetry in French: *Élegie d'Ihpétonga* (*Suivie de Masques de Cendre*), *Les Georgiques Parisiennes* and the *Chansons malaises*; this involvement with Goll's work provided the pretext for Claire Goll's accusations of plagiarism.
Letters 34, 36

Hamm, Peter (b. 1937)
Poet, literary and music critic. He was in personal contact with Nelly Sachs from 1957
Letters 11, *14,* 19, 21

Hepner, Julius
German-speaking attorney who acted for Nelly Sachs in Stockholm
Letters 50, 63

Hilty, Rudolf (b. 1925)
Swiss writer and publicist, editor of the journal *Hortulus* (St. Gallen 1951-1961), in which Nelly Sachs and Paul Celan both published work. At the prize-giving in Meersburg, he gave the official eulogy [Laudatio] for Nelly Sachs.
Letters 31, 38

Holmqvist, Bengt (b. 1924)
Finland-Swedish literary critic who was in contact with Nelly Sachs from 1950. Editor of the *Buch der Nelly Sachs* and, with his wife, of a volume of papers from the Sachs estate, *Suche nach Lebenden.*
Letters 76, 102, 103, 104

Holmqvist, Margaretha, née Lindblom (b. 1926)
Finland-Swedish translator, married to Bengt Holmqvist. Translated dramatic scenes by Nelly Sachs and co-edited the volume *Suche nach Lebenden* with her husband.
Letters 102, 104

Horowitz, Jakob (1901-1975)
Hebrew author; Nelly Sachs got to know him when he was cultural attaché at the Israeli embassy in Stockholm. Paul Celan met him in Tel-Aviv during his visit to Israel in Fall, 1969.
Letter 123

Ivarsson, Astrid
Nurse. A Stockholm acquaintance of Nelly Sachs, who lived with her for a time during the summer of 1960.
Letter 52

Israel ben Eliezer (c. 1700-1760)
Jewish mystic, founder of Hasidism
Letter 66

Josephson, Gunnar
Head of the Jewish community in Stockholm and in that capacity the landlord of the house at Bergsundsstrand 23 where Nelly Sachs lived.
Letter 70

Juster, Kurt
Journalist, among other things reporter from Sweden for the German-Jewish weekly *Aufbau* (New York)
Letter 36

Kasack, Hermann (1896-1966)
German author. 1953-1963 president of the German Akademie für Sprache und Dichtung
Letter 8

Kraft, Werner (1896-1991)
German-Jewish author, emigrated to Jerusalem in 1933
Letter 20

Leiser, Erwin (b. 1923)
Publicist and film director, emigrated to Sweden in 1938. Author of the documentary film "Mein Kampf" (1960) about the Third Reich. Editor and co-translator of a volume of selected poems by Nelly Sachs. On the occasion of a meeting with him in on 1.12.1964, Paul Celan jotted in his notebook: "Erwin Leiser with his — Jewish — wife. From four in the afternoon until half-past-twelve in the morning. [Spoke] about liberal antisemitism, left-wing anti-semitism, Enzensberger (Büchner-speech), Nelly Sachs — "it may be that the destiny of the people is illuminated in me" — and much else*. — Good impression. Gave him the Meridian. They both liked Gisèle's etchings very much. They want to speak about them with Daniel Keel in Zürich. Ask Leiser to give regards to Margarete Susman.
* Also for example about Group 47 and Horst Mönnich's Hitler Poems"
Letters 18, 19

Lennartsson, Ẹva-Lisa (b. 1910)
Swedish reciter, friend of Nelly Sachs from 1956. In 1960 she accompanied Nelly Sachs to Zurich, Meersburg, Ascona and Paris.
Letters 29, 31, 34, 38, 42, 43, 45, 72, 75, 113, 114

Lestrange, Odette de (1897-1988)
Mother of Gisèle Celan-Lestrange
Letter 75

Lortholary, Bernard
French expert on German literature and translator, student of Celan at the École Normale Supérieur. he translated poems by Nelly Sachs, including those published in L'Éphémère (Paris) under commission from Celan.
Letters 118, 120

Luria, Isaak ben Salomon (1534-1572)
Jewish mystic, cabbalist who had a strong influence on the Hasidism of eastern Europe.
Letter *16*

Margul-Sperber, Alfred (1898-1967)
German-jewish poet from the Bukovina, who promoted Paul Celan, especially during his Bucarest period (1945-47). Numerous early manuscripts of poems and translations by Celan can be found in his papers, now housed in the Bucarest Literature Museum.
Letter *82*

Mårtens, Sten
Doctor who treated Nelly Sachs at the psychiatric clinic Beckomberga, and after 1968 in the Rålombshov Hospital.
Letters 68, 95, *112*, 114, 115

Pergament, Moses (1893-1977)
Composer and music critic, earlier sponsor of Nelly Sachs. He composed an opera on the basis of her *Eli* (first performed 1959). Nelly Sachs, however, felt that the opera revealed a complete misunderstanding of her intentions.
Letters 13, 31

Pergament, Ilse, née Kutzleb (1906-1960)
Long-time friend of Nelly Sachs, married to Moses Pergament.
Letter 31

Peyer, Rudolf (b. 1929)
Swiss poet and publicist. He lived 1956-1959 in Paris, where he made the acquaintance of Paul Celan; in 1959 Celan helped to arrange a meeting between him and Nelly Sachs in Stockholm.
Letters 14, 15, 16, 17, 31

Picon, Gaëtan (1915-1976)
French writer. Co-editor of the journal *L'Éphémère* (Paris)
Letter 118

Reinert, Werner (b. 1922)
Poet; Nelly Sachs helped him to get work published in *Botteghe Oscure* (Rome).
Letter 17

Riwkin, Anna (1908-1970)
Swedish photographer, took numerous photographs of Nelly Sachs. Married to Daniel Brick.
Letters 28, 61

Rothmann, Lenke (b. 1929)
Hungarian-swedish painter, came to Sweden in 1945 after her release from a concentration camp. She was friendly with Nelly Sachs from 1951.
Letters 11, 113

Sachs, Margarete (1871-1950)
Mother of Nelly Sachs, who fled with her from Germany to Sweden and cared for her — in very cramped conditions — until her death.
Letters 17, 43, 50, 70

Scholem, Gershom (1897-1982)
Jewish philosopher of religion. Nelly Sachs (from 1950) and Paul Celan (from 1957) owned his translation of the Zohar (*Die Geheimnisse der Schöpfung. Ein Kapitel aus dem Zohar*, Berlin, 1935). Scholem's work *Die jüdische Mystik in ihren Hauptströmingen* (Frankfurt, 1957) can also be found among the Stockholm papers.
Letter *16*

Sellner, Rudolf (1905-1989)
Director of the Hessische Landestheater in Darmstadt, also from 1961 until 1972 of the Deutsche Oper in Berlin. He became acquainted with Nelly Sachs in 1957.
Letter 5

Socard, Gilbert
French writer and translator. Translated works by Nelly Sachs (in *Documents*, Paris/Cologne)
Letter *32*

Trotzig, Brigitta (b. 1929)
Swedish writer, who lived in France from 1954 until 1969.
Letter 11

Waern, Inge
Actress, Stockholm friend of Nelly Sachs. Nelly Sachs introduced her to Paul Celan. In July and August 1960, she informed Celan of the grave deterioration in Nelly Sachs's condition.
Letters 30, 49, 52, 72, 75

Weber, Werner (b. 1919)
Swiss writer and literary critic. Editor 1951-1973 of the literary desk of the *Neue Zürcher Zeitung*, where both Nelly Sachs and Paul Celan published on many occasions. He presented the eulogy [Laudatio] to Nelly Sachs at the presentation of the Peace Prize of the German Book Industry in Frankfurt.
Letters 45, 47

Wosk, Rosi
Hungarian born, came to Sweden in 1945 after being released from concentration camp. Neighbour of Nelly Sachs in the house at Bergsundsstrand 23.
Letters 55, 58, 72, 75

Chronology

Nelly Sachs	*Paul Celan*
December 10, 1891 in Berlin: birth of Leonie Sachs, only child of Margarete and the manufacturer William Sachs.	
1897-1908 Education in various private schools and through private tuition	
1903-1905 First literary works	
	November 23, 1920 in Czernowitz: birth of Paul Pessach Antschel, only child of Friederike and Leo Antschel (builder)
1921 Legenden und Erzählungen (Legends and Stories)	
1929 First publication of poems in the *Vossische Zeitung*, Berlin	*1926-1938* Education at various German, Hebrew and Romanian schools until graduation
1930 Death of her father	
From 1938 onwards: attempts to emigrate to Sweden	*1938/39* Period of study in Tours (France) for preclinical medicine, completed with the so-called P.C.B. (Physics, Chemistry, Biology)
	The first extant poems date from this period
1939 Gudrun Harlan (-Dähnert) prepares a trip to Sweden to enable the emigration of Nelly Sachs and her mother	*1939* Begins to study Romance Languages at the Rumanian (*from 1940/41* the Soviet) University of Czernowitz

Nelly Sachs	*Paul Celan*
May 16, 1940 Departure for Sweden with her mother; at first they live in private accommodation	
1941 First publication of a poem in Sweden ("Abendland"), in Swedish translation	*1941* Establishment of the ghetto in Czernowitz
One-room apartment in the house at Bergsundsstrand 23 in Stockholm	
1942 First translations of Swedish poetry	*1942* Deportation of his parents to the Michailowka Camp (Ukraine); they are presumed to have died in the same year.
	1942-44 Labour Camps in Falticeni and Buzau (Rumania)
1944-1947 Translator for "Samarbetskommitté för demokratisk uppbyggnadsarbete" (Committee for Democratic Renewal)	*1944* Recommences his studies (English) at the Russian-Ukrainian University of Czernowitz
	1945 Departure for Bucharest
	1945-1947 *Lektor* (desk-editor) and Russian-Rumanian translator at the Bucharest Publisher Cartea rusa (The Russian Book)
	1946 Anton Tchekhov, *Taranii*, (first translation from the Russian into Rumanian)

Nelly Sachs	Paul Celan
1947 In den Wohnungen des Todes (*In the Dwellings of Death* — her first book to be published after the war)	*1947* Three of his earliest German poems appear in a Bucharest newspaper ("Agora") and a Romanian translation of the "Todesfuge" ("Death Fugue") is published; all of these appear under the pseudonym "Celan"
(Trans.) *Von Welle und Granit* (Of Wave and Granite)	
	In December Departure for Vienna
1948 Margarete and Nelly Sachs move into a larger one-room apartment in the house Bergsundsstrand 23, which she retains until her death	*July 1948* Departs Vienna via Innsbruck for Paris
	Der Sand aus den Urnen (*Sand from the Urns*)
	Edgar Jené und der Traum vom Traume (a prose work — *Edgar Jené and the Dream of the Dream*)
1949 Sternverdunkelung (*Eclipse of the Stars*)	*1949* Commences a degree in German Studies and General Linguistics in Paris, taking the License ès Lettres in *July 1950*
1950 The death of her mother is followed by a serious psychological crisis	
1951 Eli, Malmö	
1952 Granted Swedish nationality	*1952* Marries the graphic artist Gisèle de Lestrange
	Mohn und Gedächtnis (*Poppy-seed and Memory*)
	Takes part in the meeting of Group 47 in Niendorf
1953 Three poems appear in the French journal *Documents*	*1953* Birth of a son, François, who dies after a few days

Nelly Sachs	*Paul Celan*
1954 Beginning of their correspondence	
	1955 Von Schwelle zu Schwelle (From Threshold to Threshold)
	Birth of a son, Eric Granted French nationality
1956 (Trans.) *Aber auch diese Sonne ist heimatlos* (*But This Sun Too is Homeless*)	*1956* Literature prize of the Cultural Section in the Bundesverband der Deutschen Industrie
1957 Und Niemand weiß weiter (And No One Knows the Way Onward)	
1958 Poetry prize of the Swedish Association of Writers	
	1958 Literature prize of the Free Hanseatic City of Bremen
(Trans.) Johannes Edfelt, *Der Schattenfischer* (*The Fisher of Shadows*)	(Trans.) Arthur Rimbaud, *Das trunkene Schiff* (*The Drunken Boat*)
First broadcast of the radio version of *Eli* written at the suggestion of Alfred Andersch (5.21.1958)	
1959 First performance of the opera version of *Eli* by Moses Pergament is followed by a serious psychological crisis	*1959* Instructor at the École Normale Supérieure
Flucht und Verwandlung (*Flight and Metamorphosis*)	
	Sprachgitter (*Bars of Language*)

Nelly Sachs	*Paul Celan*
Literature prize of the Federal Association of German Industry (Bundesverband der deutschen Industrie); she does not travel to Germany to receive the award	(Trans.) Osip Mandelstam, *Gedichte* (*Poems*)
	1960 (Trans.) Paul Valéry, *Le jeune Parque* (*The Young Fate*)
	In May Claire Goll publishes an article in the periodical *Baubudenpoet* that triggers a campagne of defamation against the designated Büchner-Prize-winner. Her accusations refer to alleged plagiarism from volumes of poetry in French by Yvan Goll that Celan had translated. The champagne, which Celan himself refers to as "infamy," deeply shocks him and leaves a permanent imprint.

25-27 May: first meeting in Zurich; Nelly Sachs travels on *May 27* to Meersburg, Paul Celan departs on *May 28* for Paris

May 29, 1960 Receives the Droste-Prize of the City of Meersburg

June 2-13: in Ascona at the invitation of Alfred Andersch

June 13-17: Nelly Sachs visits Paul Celan and his family in Paris

June 17: returns to Stockholm

Nelly Sachs	*Paul Celan*
A serious psychological crisis leads to her admission to the psychiatric department of the Sjödersjukhuset (hospital in Stockholm) on *August 8*	
	September 1-7: Paul Celan visits Nelly Sachs in Stockholm, where she either refuses to see him or does not recognize him
Transferral to the Psychiatric Clinic Beckomberga	
Beginning of October Nelly Sachs resumes contact with the outside world	*October 26* The Georg Büchner Prize is awarded to Celan in Darmstadt, where he gives an address entitled "The Meridian"
In December: provisional discharge from the psychiatric clinic into the convalescent home Högberga	
Further extensive periods in hospital until 1963	
1961 Fahrt ins Staublose (*Journey into a Dustless Realm*)	*1961* (Trans.) Sergei Esenin, *Gedichte* (*Poems*)
1962 *Zeichen im Sand* (*Signs in the Sand*)	
(Trans.) Gunnar Ekelöf, *Poesie* (*Poetry*)	
1963 Ausgewählte Gedichte (*Selected Poems*) — with the first cycle of the "Glühenden Rätsel" (*Glowing Riddles*)	*1963 Die Niemandsrose* (*The No One's Rose*)

Nelly Sachs	*Paul Celan*
(Trans.) Erik Lindegren, *Weil unser einziges Nest unsere Flügel sind* (*Because Our Wings Are Our Only Nest*)	
1964 Takes part in a meeting of Group 47 in Sigunta/Sweden	*1964* Celan is awarded the Senior Art Prize (Großer Kunstpreis) of the State of Nordrhein-Westfalen.
Glühende Rätsel (*Glowing Enigmas*) — containing the first two cycles	
1965 Nelly Sachs travels to Frankfurt to accept the Peace Prize of the German Book Industry; this is followed by her first and only visit after the war to the city of her birth. She returns as an honorary citizen of the city of Berlin	*1965* *Atemkristall* (*Breath-Crystal*), with eight etchings by Gisèle Celan-Lestrange
Späte Gedichte (*Late Poems*) — with cycles I-III of "Glowing Enigmas"	
(Trans.) *Schwedische Gedichte* (*Swedish Poems*)	
(Trans.) Karl Vennberg, *Poesie* (*Poetry*)	
1966 Die Suchende (*The Searcher*)	
December 10 The Nobel Prize for Literature is awarded to Josef S. Agnon and Nelly Sachs	

Nelly Sachs	*Paul Celan*
1967 Heart attack in March	*1967* After a serious psychiatric crisis at the beginning of the year and extensive treatment in a clinic, Celan decides, in agreement with his wife Gisèle, to move out of their shared apartment in the Rue de Longchamp because of the poor condition of his health
	Moves into the Rue Tournefort
	In July: Meeting with Martin Heidegger
	Atemwende (Turn of Breath)
	(Trans.) William Shakespeare, *Einundzwanzig Sonette* (Twenty-One Sonnets)
1968 Re-admission to a psychiatric clinic (Rålambshov Hospital)	*1968* He closely follows the events of May 1968 in Paris with enthusiasm at first, then with growing scepticism
	Celan becomes co-editor of the French literary journal *L'Éphémère,* to which he asks Nelly Sachs to contribute poems
	(Trans.) André du Bouchet, *Vakante Glut* (Incandescent Vacuum)
	(Trans.) Jules Supervielle, *Gedichte* (Poems)

Nelly Sachs	*Paul Celan*
	(Trans.) Giuseppe Ungaretti, *Das verheißene Land. Das Merkbuch des Alten* (*The Promised Land. The Old Man's Notebook*)
	Fadensonnen (*Thread-Suns*)
1969 Operation for cancer at the beginning of the year, further periods in the clinic during subsequent months; she becomes bedridden and suffers from serious pains	*1969 Scharzmaut* (*Black Toll*), with 15 etchings by Gisèle Celan-Lestrange
	September 30 - October 17 Journey to Israel, where (presumably on *Oct. 14*) he gives his "Address to the Association of Hebrew Writers"
	In November: Moves into the apartment in Avenue Emile Zola
In December: Last contacts by letter	In December: Last contacts by letter
	1970, in March Gives a reading at a meeting of the Hölderlin Society in Stuttgart
	Around 20 April Suicide in the River Seine
May 12, 1970 Nelly Sachs dies in Stockholm